THE
FASTING
Companion

Copyright © 2024 by Dr. Thando Sibanda

Published by Four Rivers Media

All rights reserved. No portion of this book may be reproduced, stored in a retrieval system, or transmitted in any form or by any means—electronic, mechanical, photocopy, recording, scanning, or other—except for brief quotations in critical reviews or articles, without prior written permission of the author.

Unless otherwise specified, all Scripture quotations are taken from the Holy Bible, New International Version®, NIV®. Copyright © 1973, 1978, 1984, 2011 by Biblica, Inc.™ Used by permission of Zondervan. All rights reserved worldwide. www.zondervan.com. The "NIV" and "New International Version" are trademarks registered in the United States Patent and Trademark Office by Biblica, Inc.™ | Scripture quotations marked ESV are from The ESV® Bible (The Holy Bible, English Standard Version®), copyright © 2001 by Crossway, a publishing ministry of Good News Publishers. Used by permission. All rights reserved. | Scripture quotations marked NKJV are taken from the New King James Version®. Copyright © 1982 by Thomas Nelson. Used by permission. All rights reserved.

For foreign and subsidiary rights, contact the author.

Cover design by Sara Young
Cover photo by Shift Focus Photography

ISBN: 978-1-964794-30-3   1 2 3 4 5 6 7 8 9 10

Printed in the United States of America

THE
FASTING
Companion

Your ultimate daily guide to a successful fast:
Unveiling Spiritual Benefits with Scientific Insights.

DR. THANDO SIBANDA

The Ideal 21-day Fasting Turnkey Strategy for
Individual and Corporate Fasts

THE IDEAL SPEAKER FOR YOUR NEXT EVENT!

Any organization that wants to develop its people to win in this area needs to hire **Dr. Thando** for a keynote and/or workshop training!

To Contact or Book **Dr. Thando Sibanda** to Speak:
bookings@drthando.com
1-469-967-9089

THE IDEAL COACH (OR CONSULTANT) FOR YOU!

If you're ready to overcome challenges, have major breakthroughs, and achieve higher levels in fasting protocols, then you will love having **Dr. Thando Sibanda** as your coach!

TO CONTACT
Dr. Thando Sibanda
Email: coaching@drthando.com

To my mother, Rev. Alice Sibanda, an apostle of prayer and fasting. You instilled this timeless and life-shifting discipline in all your children, and we are the living outcomes of your unwavering commitment.

CONTENTS

Prelude xv
Introduction 17

CHAPTER 1. **UNDERSTANDING FASTING** 19
    DAY 1
CHAPTER 2. **A NEW BEGINNING** 29
    DAY 2
CHAPTER 3. **THE PROCESS OF SURRENDER** 39
    DAY 3
CHAPTER 4. **TRUST IN GOD'S PROVISION** 49
    DAY 4
CHAPTER 5. **STRENGTH IN WEAKNESS** 59
    DAY 5
CHAPTER 6. **THE POWER OF PRAYER** 69
    DAY 6
CHAPTER 7. **EMBRACING THE SPIRITUAL JOURNEY** 79
    DAY 7
CHAPTER 8. **RESTING IN GOD'S PRESENCE** 89
    DAY 8
CHAPTER 9. **PERSEVERING THROUGH CHALLENGES** 99
    DAY 9
CHAPTER 10. **CULTIVATING SPIRITUAL DISCERNMENT** 109
    DAY 10
CHAPTER 11. **STANDING FIRM IN SPIRITUAL WARFARE** 119
    DAY 11
CHAPTER 12. **CULTIVATING A SPIRIT OF GRATITUDE** 129
    DAY 12
CHAPTER 13. **EMBRACING HUMILITY** 139

DAY 13
CHAPTER 14. **DEEPENING YOUR PRAYER LIFE** 149

DAY 14
CHAPTER 15. **ELEVATING YOUR WORSHIP** 159

DAY 15
CHAPTER 16. **THE POWER OF INTERCESSION** 169

DAY 16
CHAPTER 17. **THE FREEDOM OF SURRENDER** 181

DAY 17
CHAPTER 18. **ATTUNING TO GOD'S VOICE** 191

DAY 18
CHAPTER 19. **THE STRENGTH OF PERSEVERANCE**.......... 201

DAY 19
CHAPTER 20. **THE GIFT OF RENEWAL**...................... 211

DAY 20
CHAPTER 21. **THE GRACE OF GRATITUDE**................. 221

DAY 21
CHAPTER 22. **REFLECTION AND CELEBRATION** 231

CHAPTER 23. **PREPARING FOR RE-ENTRY** 241
CHAPTER 24. **A NEW BEGINNING** 249
CHAPTER 25. **POST-FAST REFLECTIONS AND NEXT STEPS** . .257

PRELUDE

Fasting is one of the most profound spiritual disciplines available to believers. It is an ancient practice that has the power to bring us closer to God, sharpen our spiritual senses, and unlock amazing benefits in our physical bodies. Yet, for many, the journey of fasting can be daunting—filled with challenges, uncertainties, and the potential for physical discomfort. This is where *The Fasting Companion* comes in—a tool designed to guide you, encourage you, and support you throughout your fasting journey, whether you are undertaking a personal fast or participating in a corporate fast.

The Fasting Companion is more than just a book; it is your daily guide, your mentor, and your source of encouragement as you embark on this sacred journey. Each chapter is thoughtfully crafted to provide you with the spiritual nourishment you need to stay focused and persevere, regardless of the challenges you may face. The book is structured to lead you day by day, helping you to navigate the physical, emotional, and spiritual aspects of fasting with wisdom and grace.

One of the most powerful aspects of this book is the insights it offers. As you journey through each day, you will find scriptures that speak directly to the heart of your experience, prayer prompts that guide you in deepening your conversation with God, and scientific insights that help you understand what is happening to your body and mind as you fast. This holistic approach ensures that you are not just fasting for the sake of it, but that you are engaging in a process that transforms you from the inside out.

The advantages of following *The Fasting Companion* day by day are immense. By committing to this process, you are giving yourself the opportunity to experience the fullness of what fasting has to offer. You are creating space in your life for God to work in powerful ways, reveal His will, and bring about spiritual breakthroughs that can only come through this disciplined practice. Whether you are fasting for personal reasons—seeking clarity, strength, or spiritual renewal—or as part of a corporate fast with your church or community, this book will be an invaluable resource.

What makes *The Fasting Companion* truly special is its ability to meet you where you are, offering encouragement when you feel weak, wisdom when you face challenges, and celebration as you reach milestones in your fasting journey. The book is designed to be interactive, inviting you to reflect, pray, and journal as you go. This engagement deepens your experience, making each day of the fast a meaningful step toward greater spiritual maturity.

As you begin this journey, know that you are not alone. The pages of *The Fasting Companion* are filled with the wisdom of those who have walked this path before you, who understand the trials and the triumphs of fasting. This book is here to support you, guide you, and help you make the most of this sacred time.

May this journey draw you closer to God, strengthen your faith, and leave you transformed by His grace.

With blessings and encouragement,
Dr. Thando Sibanda

INTRODUCTION

Welcome to a journey that is as ancient as it is transformative. Fasting is not just a discipline—it's a path I have walked my entire life. Born into a Christian family where fasting and prayer were the heartbeat of our spiritual practice, I was immersed in this journey from a young age. My mother, Alice, would embark on twenty-one-day fasts with only water, setting an example for my siblings and me. We learned early on that fasting wasn't just about abstaining from food; it was about drawing closer to God, finding clarity in life, and experiencing a renewal of the mind, body, and spirit.

This journey is not theoretical for me. It's not an instruction from afar. Over the years, I've completed numerous twenty-one-day fasts, each one revealing more of the whispers of the soul, the depths, sights, and sounds of the Spirit that can only be experienced when we silence the noise of the physical world. I remember the tug of war between my mind clamoring for sustenance while my spirit grew stronger, clearer, and more alive with every passing day. I've walked this path, and I invite you to walk it with me.

This is a journey of regeneration. In nature, we see how God has embedded codes of renewal into life itself. Eagles pluck out their old feathers and beaks to make way for new growth. Snakes shed their old skin to reveal new life.

And humans? We fast. Fasting is our path of shedding, of letting go of the old to make room for the new. It's more than just abstinence from food; it's a spiritual, mental, and physical renewal in every sense.

Over the next twenty-one days, this companion will be your guide, offering you insights, wisdom, and practical tools to walk this path successfully. While this book is structured around a twenty-one-day fast, the principles can be adapted to any length of fasting. Whether you're a seasoned faster or embarking on this journey for the first time, know this: the rewards are abundant. Your spirit will be sharpened, your mind renewed, and your body rejuvenated.

So, I invite you to come along with me on this sacred journey. Together, we will walk through the valleys of hunger and emerge on the mountaintops of revelation. Let's find the renewal God has set aside for us. Let's uncover the deeper truths that await beyond the physical realm. This is your companion, and I am honored to walk alongside you.

Welcome to the journey. Let the fast begin.

CHAPTER 1

UNDERSTANDING FASTING
Biblical Foundations and Scientific Benefits

Fasting is more than just abstaining from food; it's an invitation—a sacred, transformative journey where your spiritual life, mental resilience, and physical body are intertwined in surrender and renewal. Welcome to *The Fasting Companion*. Together, we will walk through every day of your twenty-one-day fast, breaking down the shifts in your body, guiding your prayers, and exploring the profound spiritual impact of fasting.

Think of this journey as a time to reset—not just physically, but spiritually and emotionally. As we begin, let's establish a foundation by exploring both the biblical roots of fasting and the incredible scientific benefits that accompany it. Whether this is your first fast or one of many, this chapter will equip you with the understanding and motivation you need to start strong.

A SACRED PRACTICE OF SURRENDER

Fasting, as seen in the Bible, is a profound act of worship, surrender, and humility before God. It's not merely a physical denial of food; it's about creating sacred space for God to move, speak, and transform. The Bible is filled with stories that reveal the power and purpose of fasting.

Think of Moses on Mount Sinai. In Exodus 34:28, Moses fasted for forty days and nights as he received the Ten Commandments. This wasn't just skipping meals; it was a total commitment to God's will. Moses's fast was an act of consecration, aligning himself with God's purpose for the Israelites. He was sustained not by physical food but by spiritual sustenance—God's presence and His word.

We also see the power of fasting in the Book of Esther. When Queen Esther learned of the plan to annihilate the Jewish people, she called for a three-day fast—not just for herself but for all the Jews in Susa (Esther 4:16). This fast was a plea for divine intervention, a cry for deliverance. Through fasting, Esther's people were saved, reminding us that fasting is a powerful weapon in spiritual warfare.

Even Jesus Himself fasted for forty days in the wilderness before His public ministry began (Matthew 4:1-2). In this time of fasting, He prepared for the monumental task ahead, resisting the temptations of Satan and drawing strength from His dependence on God. His fast was not just about discipline; it was a profound declaration of His reliance on God, setting an example for us all.

These biblical stories reveal that fasting is deeply connected to spiritual breakthroughs, divine guidance, and preparation for significant tasks. Fasting is an invitation to draw closer to God, lean on Him more fully, and align ourselves with His will.

A TOOL FOR SPIRITUAL BREAKTHROUGH

Fasting's significance goes beyond the physical act; its outcomes are deeply spiritual. In Isaiah 58, the prophet reveals God's heart for fasting: "Is not this the kind of fasting I have chosen: to loose the chains of injustice and untie the cords of the yoke, to set the oppressed free and break every yoke?" (Isaiah 58:6).

Isaiah underscores that fasting, when approached with the right heart, brings about justice, freedom, and healing. It is a spiritual tool that God uses to initiate transformation in both our lives and the world around us. Fasting is not just about personal piety—it's about partnering with God in His redemptive work.

This is why fasting often precedes great moves of God. Before the walls of Jericho fell, Joshua and the Israelites consecrated themselves (Joshua 3:5). Before the disciples received the Holy Spirit at Pentecost, they spent time in prayer and fasting (Acts 1:14). And before Paul and Barnabas were sent out on their missionary journey, the church in Antioch fasted and prayed (Acts 13:2-3).

Fasting prepares our hearts for what God is about to do. It creates an atmosphere of expectation, where we are more attuned to God's voice and open to His leading. As you embark on this twenty-one-day journey, remember that you are engaging in a practice that has shaped history. You are stepping into a sacred tradition that holds the power to bring about profound change.

THE SCIENCE OF FASTING: **UNDERSTANDING WHAT'S HAPPENING IN YOUR BODY**

Now that we've laid a biblical foundation for fasting, it's time to shift our focus to the incredible changes happening inside your body. Fasting is a journey of faith, but it's also a journey through your own physical biology, with a process more profound than we often realize. You see, while the spiritual benefits of fasting are immense, the physical benefits are equally remarkable—and understanding them will help you appreciate this practice even more.

When you fast, your body enters a unique state of renewal, where it begins to heal, repair, and regenerate. Let's take this journey one step at a time, beginning with what's happening inside your body as you fast. For the sake of consistency throughout the book, we will begin by defining key words that describe the scientific processes happening in our bodies during a fast.

KEYWORD DEFINITION: AUTOPHAGY

Autophagy is like your body's natural recycling system—it's the process through which cells clean up and break down damaged parts, renewing themselves and making room for fresh, healthy components. During fasting, autophagy becomes more active because, without a constant supply of food, the body shifts its focus to self-repair and renewal. Think of it as your cells' way of tidying up and removing old and potentially harmful material, which supports cellular health, longevity, and resilience.[1]

For a more in-depth look at autophagy, refer to the source listed at the end of this book.

Fasting initiates a biological process called autophagy—a kind of cellular cleanup crew that springs into action when your body goes without food for a certain period of time. Think of it as a deep clean for your cells. Damaged cells, old proteins, and other debris get swept away, making room for fresh, healthy cells. This process is linked to greater longevity and protection against diseases like cancer and Alzheimer's. Dr. Yoshinori Ohsumi, a Japanese cell biologist, was awarded the Nobel Prize in 2016 for his discoveries about how autophagy works. His research showed that fasting triggers autophagy, allowing your body to remove toxins from your cells, repair damaged DNA, and improve overall cellular function. During longer fasts, like the twenty-one-day fast you're about to embark on, autophagy is even more active, creating space for real, deep renewal at the cellular level.[2]

But that's not all. Fasting also balances your blood sugar and increases insulin sensitivity, which is crucial for maintaining energy and preventing long-term health issues. As you fast, your body switches from burning glucose (sugar) for energy to burning fat—this is called ketosis. When your body enters ketosis, you start producing ketones, which fuel your brain with

---

1 Noboru Mizushima and Beth Levine, "Autophagy in Human Diseases," *The New England Journal of Medicine* 383, no. 16 (2020): 1564-76, https://doi.org/10.1056/NEJMra2022774.
2 The Nobel Prize in Physiology or Medicine, "Press Release," The Nobel Prize, Oct. 3, 2016.

a cleaner, more efficient source of energy. This results in sharper focus, better mental clarity, and a feeling of heightened awareness. Moreover, fasting lowers inflammation—one of the key contributors to chronic conditions like heart disease, diabetes, and arthritis. By reducing these inflammatory markers, your body heals in ways that extend far beyond the visible. Fasting isn't just about what you stop doing (eating); it's about how your body transforms in response.

THE MENTAL AND EMOTIONAL IMPACT

KEYWORD DEFINITION: BRAIN-DERIVED NEUROTROPHIC FACTOR (BDNF)

Brain-derived neurotrophic factor, or BDNF, is a special protein in your brain that helps neurons grow and stay healthy. Think of BDNF as "brain fertilizer"—it promotes the survival and growth of brain cells, supports new neural connections, and plays a crucial role in learning, memory, and mood regulation. During fasting, BDNF levels can increase, which may improve mental clarity, resilience to stress, and cognitive function. BDNF also helps protect the brain from degeneration, making it a key factor in long-term brain health.

For a more detailed exploration of BDNF, refer to the source listed at the end of this book.

While your body adjusts to fasting, there are changes happening in your mind and emotions, too. It's normal to feel hunger, irritability, or fatigue in the beginning. But these are temporary discomforts, like a fog that lifts. Once your body adjusts, you'll find greater mental clarity, emotional stability, and a renewed sense of calm. A study showed that fasting boosts the production of brain-derived neurotrophic factor (BDNF), a protein that promotes the growth and survival of neurons. Higher levels of BDNF have been linked to improved mood, enhanced memory, and a lower risk of anxiety and depression.[3] In other words, fasting can act as a reset for your brain, supporting your mental health and boosting your emotional well-being.

But the mental benefits go even deeper. Fasting removes one of life's greatest distractions—food—giving your mind the freedom to focus more fully on spiritual matters. Without the interruptions of eating and digestion, many find their prayers more focused, their meditation more profound, and their connection with God more tangible. The longer you fast, the more you'll notice a heightened sense of awareness, like the veil between you and the spiritual world is thinner.

THE SPIRITUAL SIGNIFICANCE OF PHYSICAL BENEFITS

You might be wondering—what does all this science have to do with the spiritual side of fasting? Actually, they are deeply connected. The Bible tells us that our bodies are the temple of the Holy Spirit (1 Corinthians 6:19). When we fast, we're not only caring for our spiritual well-being, but we're tending to the very temple where God dwells. The physical benefits of fasting—cellular repair, mental clarity, reduced inflammation—are all part of God's incredible design for our holistic health. The healing happening in your body mirrors the spiritual cleansing and renewal God desires for your soul. Just as fasting removes toxins from your cells, it also removes spiritual and emotional toxins, clearing the way for God to work more deeply in your life. This journey of fasting is a reminder that God cares about every part of us—body, mind, and spirit. When you fast, you're not just depriving yourself of food; you're creating space for God to nourish you in ways you may never have imagined.

---

[3] Refat Alkurd et al., "Effect of calorie restriction and intermittent fasting regimens on BDNF levels and cognitive function in humans: A systematic review," *Medicina* 57 (2021): 1-20, https://doi.org/10.3390/xxxx.

PREPARING FOR YOUR FAST

SETTING YOUR INTENTIONS
Before you begin your fast, take a moment to reflect. What is God calling you to focus on during this time? Are you seeking deeper intimacy with Him? Do you need clarity or breakthrough in a specific area? Are you fasting for healing, guidance, or transformation? Whatever it is, take some time to pray and ask God to reveal His purposes for your fast. Write them down in a journal or on a piece of paper that you can return to when you need encouragement along the way.

PREPARING YOUR BODY
Fasting, especially for extended periods, can be a challenge for your body if you are not used to it, but with the right preparation and direction, you can ease the transition. In the days leading up to your fast, begin cutting back on sugar, caffeine, and processed foods to reduce withdrawal symptoms. Drink plenty of water and keep yourself hydrated before, during, and after the fast. Hydration is key to keeping your energy levels up and supporting your body's detoxification process. Remember to be kind to yourself. You're not fasting to punish your body, but to bring it into alignment with your spirit. Gentle exercise like walking or stretching is great for keeping your body moving without overtaxing your energy reserves. The goal is to support your physical body while focusing on your spiritual journey.

PREPARING YOUR SPIRIT
Lastly, take time to prepare your spirit. Spend time in prayer, asking God to guide you, sustain you, and strengthen you for the journey ahead. Remember that fasting is not about earning God's favor—it's about drawing closer to Him.

Incorporate other spiritual practices into your routine, such as longer periods of prayer, reading Scripture, and moments of stillness.

YOUR FASTING TOOLKIT

Before embarking on your twenty-one-day fasting journey, it's essential to prepare yourself both spiritually and practically. Fasting can be a profound spiritual experience, but it also requires careful attention to your physical well-being. The tools you'll need for this fast will help you monitor your health, create a space for spiritual growth, and maintain focus throughout the journey. Here is a list of recommended items to equip yourself with before you begin your fast:

FASTING TOOLKIT

1) Bible—Your source of spiritual nourishment and wisdom throughout the fast.
2) Journal—Document your thoughts, revelations, and prayer reflections each day.
3) Purified Water—Hydration is key during a fast. Ensure you have enough purified water to last through your fasting period, especially if you are retreating.
4) Glucose Monitor—A handy tool to monitor your blood sugar levels, especially during longer fasts.
5) Blood Pressure Monitor—Keep track of your blood pressure, particularly if you have a history of hypertension.
6) Weight Scale—While fasting isn't about weight loss, this tool can help monitor any significant changes in body weight.
7) Notepad and Pen—Keep these handy for additional notes, scriptures, or prayer prompts.

8) Herbal Tea and Honey—In case of low blood sugar, herbal tea with a bit of honey can provide a gentle lift.
9) Daily Environment Free of Distraction—Create a quiet, peaceful space to focus on your prayer and spiritual reflection.
10) Time for Solitude—If you're working during the fast, make time during breaks to enter solitude and meditate.

You can easily find these tools at your local grocery store. It's a good idea to stock up on water and other essentials before starting, particularly if you plan on retreating or limiting movement during your fast. Measure your vitals daily and keep a log of your progress. You can also keep track of this process on the Fasting Companion app (TFC), downloadable from the Google Play Store and the Apple Store.

Disclaimer: If you are on prescription medication or pregnant, please consult a physician before engaging in a long fasting protocol like the twenty-one-day fast.

By preparing your fasting toolkit, you ensure that your journey will be safe, focused, and as impactful as possible.

EMBRACING THE JOURNEY

You're about to embark on a twenty-one-day fast, and the path ahead may have its ups and downs. But through it all, remember that fasting is not about achieving perfection—it's about surrendering to God's process of renewal. Some days will feel easy, while others may challenge you. But in both, God is working, drawing you closer to Him. Use this book as your companion, your guide. Remember that the physical, mental, and spiritual benefits of fasting are deeply connected, and you're about to experience a powerful transformation that will impact every part of your life. Keep your eyes fixed on Jesus, knowing that He will sustain you through each step of this journey.

Let's begin together. This is a path worth walking, and I'm honored to walk it with you.

CHAPTER 2

DAY 1

A NEW BEGINNING

EMBRACING THE START OF YOUR FAST

Welcome to Day 1 of your twenty-one-day fasting journey! Today marks the beginning of a transformative process that will impact not only your spiritual life but also your mind and body. Starting a fast can feel both exciting and daunting. You may be filled with anticipation for what God will do in your life over the next three weeks, but you might also be wondering how you'll manage without the regular rhythms of eating.

Take a deep breath and remind yourself that you are not alone on this journey. God is with you, and He is inviting you into a deeper relationship with Him. Fasting is a time to disconnect from the world's distractions and draw closer to the heart of God. It's a sacred time of renewal, and today, you are taking the first step.

> **OVERVIEW OF DAY 1: SETTING THE FOUNDATION**

Day 1 is all about laying the foundation for your fast. Just as a building needs a solid foundation to stand strong, your fast requires a firm spiritual and mental grounding. Today is a day to set your intentions, seek God's presence, and begin with a heart full of expectancy.

Fasting is as much a mental and emotional journey as it is a physical one. Your mindset today will set the tone for the days ahead. Approach this fast with a heart of surrender and an open mind, ready to receive whatever God has in store for you. Remember, fasting is not about earning God's favor or proving your spiritual strength; it's about aligning yourself with God's will and creating space for His Spirit to work in you.

> **SCRIPTURE OF THE DAY: MATTHEW 6:16-18**

When you fast, do not look somber as the hypocrites do, for they disfigure their faces to show others they are fasting. Truly I tell you, they have received their reward in full. But when you fast, put oil on your head and wash your face, so that it will not be obvious to others that you are fasting, but only to your Father, who is unseen; and your Father, who sees what is done in secret, will reward you. —Matthew 6:16-18

Jesus's teaching on fasting in the Sermon on the Mount reminds us that fasting is a deeply personal and intimate act of worship. It's not about outward appearances or gaining the approval of others; it's about drawing close to God and doing so with humility and sincerity.

As you begin your fast, reflect on these words of Jesus. He emphasizes the importance of fasting with the right heart—one that is focused on God rather than on external recognition. Let this scripture guide you as you set your intentions for the fast. Approach this time with a genuine desire to know God more deeply and to be transformed by His presence.

> **KEY THOUGHT: FASTING IS AN ACT OF OBEDIENCE AND HUMILITY.**

Today's key thought centers around the idea that fasting is an act of obedience and humility before God. In the Bible, fasting is often connected with repentance, seeking God's guidance, and preparing for significant spiritual encounters. By choosing to fast, you are placing yourself in a posture of humility, acknowledging your need for God's guidance, strength, and provision.

Fasting is a tangible way to say, "Lord, I need You more than I need anything else." It's a declaration that you are willing to set aside your physical needs to pursue a deeper spiritual connection with God. As you move through this first day, remind yourself that this fast is an act of worship and a demonstration of your commitment to God's will in your life.

> **PRAYER PROMPT: SURRENDERING YOUR FAST TO GOD**

Prayer is the lifeblood of fasting. It's what turns fasting from a mere diet into a spiritual journey. On this first day, your prayer focus is on surrendering your fast to God. Invite Him into every aspect of your fast—your thoughts, your emotions, your physical needs, and your spiritual desires.

PRAYER PROMPT:

"Father, I come before You today as I begin this fast, acknowledging that I cannot do this in my own strength. I surrender this fast to You,

Lord, I ask that You guide me, sustain me, and speak to me during this time. Help me to keep my focus on You and not on the discomfort or challenges that may come. Lord, I am fasting because I need You. I desire to draw closer to You, to hear Your voice more clearly, and to be transformed by Your presence. As I let go of physical nourishment, fill me with Your spiritual nourishment. Be my strength, my guide, and my comfort in the days ahead. In Jesus's name, I pray. Amen."

SCIENTIFIC INSIGHT: THE BEGINNING OF DETOXIFICATION

KEY WORD: DEFINITION: DETOXIFICATION

Detoxification is your body's natural cleaning service. Imagine it as a self-renewing system designed to flush out toxins and harmful substances. During fasting, this process ramps up, as your body uses stored fat and other reserves for fuel, breaking down and eliminating toxins. It's like giving your body a reset, helping it to work more efficiently.[4]

Let's talk about what's happening in your body as you begin your fast. On this first day, your body is starting to transition from its regular eating patterns into a state of fasting. Initially, you may feel hunger pangs or experience cravings as your body adjusts to the lack of food. This is completely normal and to be expected. Remember, hunger is powered by a hormone called ghrelin. If ignored, ghrelin's levels will go down in your body and the hunger pangs will subside in the days ahead.

As you refrain from eating, your body begins to tap into its glycogen stores—these are the glucose reserves stored in your liver and muscles. Glycogen provides a quick source of energy, but it only lasts for about twenty-four

---

4 "Understanding Detoxification: A Guide by the American Hospital Association," *AHA Physician Alliance*, https://www.ahaphysicianforum.org/health/understanding-detoxification-a-guide/.

to forty-eight hours. Once these stores are depleted, your body will start to switch its energy source from glucose to fat.

This process is known as ketosis, where your body begins to break down fat into ketones, which serve as an alternative fuel source. Ketosis typically begins after the first couple of days of fasting, but the transition starts now as your body begins to detoxify. During this early stage, your body is also flushing out toxins, leading to the detoxification process.

Detoxification is one of the many benefits of fasting. By giving your digestive system a break, your body can focus on cleansing itself from the inside out. This cleansing process can help to improve digestion, boost your immune system, and increase your energy levels over time. Although you might not feel these benefits immediately, trust that your body is working hard to reset and rejuvenate itself.

DAY 1 TIP: **STAY HYDRATED!**

Drinking water on the first day of your fast is essential. Water helps flush out toxins, supports your energy levels, and keeps you feeling more comfortable as your body adjusts to the change. Fasting can sometimes bring mild headaches or fatigue, especially at the beginning, and staying hydrated is a simple way to help prevent these. Aim to sip water regularly throughout the day—your body will thank you for it as it embarks on this cleansing process!

JOURNALING: **REFLECTING ON YOUR FIRST DAY**

Journaling is a powerful tool during your fasting journey. It allows you to process your thoughts, record your experiences, and track your spiritual growth. On this first day, take some time to reflect on your intentions for the fast, any emotions or physical sensations you're experiencing, and what God is speaking to you.

JOURNALING PROMPTS:

1) What are your primary intentions for this fast? Write down the reasons why you decided to embark on this twenty-one-day fast. What do you hope to achieve spiritually, mentally, and physically?

_____

_____

_____

_____

_____

_____

_____

2) How are you feeling physically and emotionally? Describe any physical sensations, such as hunger or fatigue, and any emotions that are coming up. How are you responding to these feelings?

_____

_____

_____

_____

_____

_____

_____

3) What is God saying to you today? As you pray and meditate on the Scripture, what do you sense God is speaking to your heart? Record any insights, impressions, or revelations you receive.

_____
_____
_____
_____
_____
_____
_____
_____
_____

4) What challenges do you anticipate during this fast? Consider the potential obstacles you might face over the next twenty-one days. How can you prepare yourself to overcome them?

_____
_____
_____
_____
_____
_____
_____

5) How can you stay focused on God during this fast? Write down some strategies or practices that will help you keep your focus on God, such as specific prayer times, Scripture reading, or worship.

_____
_____
_____
_____
_____
_____
_____
_____

Journaling not only helps you process your thoughts and experiences but also serves as a record of your journey that you can look back on after the fast is over. It's a way to capture the spiritual insights and breakthroughs you'll experience along the way.

ENCOURAGEMENT FOR THE JOURNEY AHEAD

As you conclude this first day, take a moment to acknowledge the step of faith you've taken. Starting a fast is no small feat; it requires courage, discipline, and a willingness to step outside of your comfort zone. But remember, you are not doing this alone. God is with you every step of the way, and He is faithful to sustain you.

Fasting is often compared to a marathon rather than a sprint. It requires endurance, patience, and persistence. There will be days when you feel strong and days when you feel weak. On the strong days, give thanks to God for His grace. On the weak days, lean into His strength, knowing that His power is made perfect in your weakness (2 Corinthians 12:9).

As you journey through these twenty-one days, keep your eyes on Jesus, the author and finisher of your faith (Hebrews 12:2). He understands what you are going through, and He is with you every step of the way. Remember, fasting is not about achieving a spiritual milestone; it's about deepening your relationship with God and allowing Him to work in and through you.

LOOKING AHEAD: **PREPARING FOR DAY 2**

Congratulations on completing Day 1 of your fast! As you prepare for tomorrow, keep in mind that the journey is just beginning. Day 2 will continue to build on the foundation you've laid today, with a focus on the process of surrender. You'll delve deeper into what it means to surrender your will to God and trust Him fully during this time.

Tonight, as you rest, pray for continued strength and grace for the days ahead. Ask God to prepare your heart for the work He wants to do in you during this fast. Remember, each day of this journey is a step closer to the breakthrough and transformation God has for you.

CHAPTER 3

DAY 2

THE PROCESS OF SURRENDER

DEEPENING YOUR COMMITMENT

Welcome to Day 2 of your fasting journey. If you're reading this, you've successfully completed the first day—a significant achievement! You may have faced some challenges, but you've also taken a crucial step toward deepening your relationship with God. Today, we will focus on the process of surrender, a key aspect of fasting that allows us to truly align with God's will.

Surrender is not a one-time act; it's an ongoing process that we must revisit each day of the fast. On this second day, you'll likely start to feel the physical effects of fasting more acutely. Hunger, fatigue, and even irritability can start to set in. These physical sensations are reminders of our dependence on God. They invite us to surrender our comforts, our control, and our cravings to Him, trusting that He will provide what we need.

Today's focus is about going deeper into this surrender, allowing God to refine your desires, shape your character, and align your heart with His purposes.

OVERVIEW OF DAY 2: EMBRACING SURRENDER

The theme for Day 2 is surrender—an essential component of fasting and spiritual growth. Fasting inherently involves surrender, as you're letting go of something you usually rely on (food) to focus more fully on God. But this surrender goes beyond just giving up meals; it's about surrendering your entire being—your thoughts, emotions, desires, and will—to God.

As you move through today, consider the areas of your life that you need to surrender to God. Are there aspects of your heart that you've been holding back? Are there fears, anxieties, or desires that you've been trying to control on your own? Today is the day to lay these at the feet of Jesus, trusting Him to take control.

SCRIPTURE OF THE DAY: PSALM 51:10

"Create in me a clean heart, O God, and renew a right spirit within me."—Psalm 51:10 (ESV)

Psalm 51 is a powerful passage of scripture that speaks to the heart of surrender. David wrote this psalm in a moment of deep repentance, recognizing his need for God's cleansing and renewal. The verse for today, Psalm 51:10, is a prayer for God to create a clean heart and renew a right spirit within us.

This verse captures the essence of what fasting is about: a desire for inner transformation. As you fast, you're asking God to do a deep work in your heart, cleansing it from impurities and renewing your spirit. This process requires surrender—letting go of your old ways, your sins, and your fears and allowing God to mold you into the person He created you to be.

As you meditate on this verse, invite God to search your heart and reveal any areas that need cleansing. Pray for the grace to surrender these areas to Him and trust in His ability to renew and restore you.

> **KEY THOUGHT:**
> **SURRENDER IS THE PATHWAY TO RENEWAL.**

Today's key thought is that surrender is the pathway to renewal. In order to experience the fullness of God's renewal in our lives, we must first be willing to surrender all that we are to Him. This surrender is not just a one-time event but a daily, ongoing process. Each day of your fast is an opportunity to surrender more of yourself to God and to allow Him to do a deeper work in you.

When you surrender, you're not giving up; you're giving in to God's greater plan for your life. You're choosing to trust Him more than you trust yourself, believing that His ways are higher than your ways (Isaiah 55:8-9). This act of surrender is what opens the door for God to bring renewal, healing, and transformation into your life.

As you move through today, keep this thought in mind: Surrender is not a loss; it's a gain. It's the key to unlocking the renewal that God desires to bring into every area of your life.

> **PRAYER PROMPT: A PRAYER OF SURRENDER**

Today's prayer focus is on surrender. Take some time to come before God in prayer, offering up every part of your life to Him. Be honest about the areas where you're struggling to let go and ask for His help in fully surrendering to His will.

PRAYER PROMPT:

"Lord, today I come before You with a heart of surrender. I acknowledge that there are areas of my life that I've been trying to control, but I know that You are the only one who truly holds my life in Your hands. I surrender my thoughts, my desires, my fears, and my plans to You. I ask that You would take control and guide me in Your ways. Create in me a clean heart, O God, and renew a right spirit within me. Help me to let go of anything that is not in line with Your will and to trust You completely. I know that surrendering to You is not a loss, but a gain—because in You, I find true life and peace. Thank You for being patient with me and for lovingly guiding me on this journey of surrender. In Jesus's name, I pray. Amen."

> ## SCIENTIFIC INSIGHT:
> ## THE BODY'S TRANSITION TO KETOSIS

KEYWORD DEFINITION: KETOSIS

Ketosis is a metabolic state where your body starts burning fat for fuel instead of glucose. When you're fasting, your glucose levels drop, so your body turns to stored fat for energy, producing molecules called ketones in the process. Ketosis is like switching from a gas car to an electric car: it's a different, more efficient fuel system for your body.[5]

On this second day of fasting, your body is continuing its transition from using glucose as its primary energy source to burning fat. This process is known as ketosis, and it's a key part of the body's adaptation to fasting.

---

[5] "Ketosis," *Cleveland Clinic*, 15 Aug. 2022, https://my.clevelandclinic.org/health/articles/24003-ketosis; Latah Nagamani Dillirag, "The Evolution of Ketosis: Potential Impact on Clinical Conditions," *Nutrients* 14, no. 17 (2022): 3613, https://doi.org/10.3390/nu14173613.

As your glycogen stores deplete (which usually happens within the first twenty-four to forty-eight hours of fasting), your body begins to break down stored fat into molecules called ketones. These ketones are then used as an alternative fuel source, especially for your brain. This shift in energy source can lead to various physical sensations, including a decrease in hunger pangs and an increase in mental clarity.

Ketosis is not just a survival mechanism; it's also associated with several health benefits. Research has shown that ketosis can help reduce inflammation, improve cognitive function, and even promote longevity. The body's ability to efficiently switch to fat metabolism during fasting is a testament to its remarkable capacity for adaptation and self-healing.

During this time, you might experience what's often referred to as the "keto flu"—a set of symptoms that can include headaches, fatigue, irritability, and dizziness. These symptoms are usually temporary and are a sign that your body is adjusting to its new fuel source. Staying hydrated, getting plenty of rest, and being gentle with yourself can help ease this transition.

Remember, your body is designed to handle this process, and these initial discomforts will likely subside as you continue fasting. Trust that your body knows what it's doing and that this transition is an important part of the cleansing and renewal process.

> DAY 2 TIP: **KEEP HYDRATION A PRIORITY**

On the second day of fasting, staying hydrated becomes even more important. As your body starts adapting to the fast, drinking plenty of water helps support your metabolism and prevents dehydration, which can sometimes make you feel sluggish or give you a headache. Water also helps curb any remaining hunger pangs by keeping your stomach full, making the transition smoother. Try to carry a bottle with you and take small sips throughout the day—this simple habit will help you stay energized and focused as you move deeper into the fasting process!

JOURNALING: **REFLECTING ON SURRENDER**

Journaling is a powerful way to process what God is doing in your heart during this time of fasting. On this second day, take some time to reflect on the theme of surrender and how it's playing out in your life.

JOURNALING PROMPTS:

1) What areas of your life are you finding difficult to surrender? Write down any specific fears, desires, or control issues that are coming to the surface. How can you begin to let go of these and trust God with them?

_____

_____

_____

_____

_____

_____

_____

2) How does the process of surrender feel to you? Are there emotions that accompany your surrender, such as relief, anxiety, or peace? How are you navigating these emotions?

_____

_____

3) In what ways do you sense God asking you to surrender more fully? Reflect on any areas where you feel God is nudging you to let go and trust Him more. What would it look like to take a step of faith in these areas?

4) How is your body responding to the fast so far? Document any physical sensations, challenges, or improvements you're noticing. How are you supporting your body through this transition?

5) What prayers of surrender are on your heart today? Write out a personal prayer of surrender, expressing your willingness to give everything to God and asking for His help in doing so.

___

Journaling helps to anchor your thoughts and emotions during this fasting journey. It provides a space for you to be honest with yourself and with God, and it serves as a record of the work that God is doing in your life.

ENCOURAGEMENT FOR THE JOURNEY AHEAD

As you conclude Day 2, remember that surrender is a process, not a destination. Each day of this fast is an opportunity to surrender a little more, let go of what you're holding onto, and allow God to work in your life in deeper ways.

Surrendering to God is not about giving up control as much as it's about giving over control to the One who knows what is best for you. It's about trusting that God's plans for your life are good, even when you can't see the full picture. As you continue to fast, keep your heart open to the ways God is leading you to surrender and be willing to follow where He leads.

God honors the heart that is surrendered to Him. In your moments of weakness, when the hunger pangs are strong or when doubts creep in, remember that surrender is not a sign of defeat but of victory in Christ. His strength is made perfect in your weakness (2 Corinthians 12:9), and He will sustain you through this journey.

LOOKING AHEAD: **PREPARING FOR DAY 3**

You've made it through the first two days of your fast—well done! Tomorrow, as you move into Day 3, the focus will be on trusting in God's provision. Fasting is a powerful way to remind yourself that God is your ultimate provider, both spiritually and physically.

As you prepare for tomorrow, spend some time in prayer, asking God to increase your faith and help you trust in His provision. Reflect on the ways He has provided for you in the past and how He continues to sustain you each day. Rest in the knowledge that He is with you, guiding you, and providing for your every need.

CHAPTER 4

DAY 3

TRUST IN GOD'S PROVISION

THE INVITATION TO TRUST

Welcome to Day 3 of your fasting journey. By now, you're beginning to feel more of the physical effects of fasting, and perhaps you've already faced some internal battles—whether it's hunger, fatigue, or simply the challenge of breaking away from your normal routine. But today, the focus shifts toward something deeper: trusting in God's provision.

As you progress through this fast, you're moving further from reliance on physical nourishment and closer to an understanding that God is your ultimate provider. It's natural to think about food, especially during a fast, but today is about more than just sustaining your body; it's about recognizing that every need you have, physical or spiritual, is met in God.

This day invites you to focus on a fundamental truth: God is the provider of everything you need. Fasting strips away the things you rely on daily, revealing where your true trust lies. And as you let go of those earthly comforts, you're given the opportunity to place your trust fully in God's capable hands.

OVERVIEW OF DAY 3: LEANING INTO GOD'S PROVISION

The theme for Day 3 is trust—specifically, trusting God as your provider. Trust can sometimes feel abstract, but during a fast, it becomes very tangible. You're trusting God not only for the physical strength to continue but also for spiritual nourishment, emotional stability, and direction for your life.

On this third day, you may feel the discomfort of hunger more intensely, and with it, the realization of how much you typically rely on food for energy, comfort, and focus. This realization is a powerful reminder that while food sustains the body, it is God who sustains your spirit. He provides for you in ways that go far beyond the physical.

As you go through today, reflect on how God has provided for you in the past, how He is providing for you now, and how He will continue to do so. Fasting opens up space in your life to recognize His provision in ways you may have overlooked before.

SCRIPTURE OF THE DAY: MATTHEW 4:4

"Jesus answered, 'It is written, Man shall not live on bread alone, but on every word that comes from the mouth of God.'"—Matthew 4:4

Today's scripture takes us to a moment when Jesus was fasting in the wilderness. After fasting for forty days, He was approached by the devil, who tempted Him to turn stones into bread. Jesus responded with these powerful words, reminding us that while physical food is necessary for survival, it is God's Word and presence that truly sustain us.

As you reflect on this verse, consider the implications for your own fast. Yes, you need food to nourish your body, but during this fast, you are choosing to feed on something even more essential—God's Word. Jesus knew that true sustenance comes from His Father, and His response in the wilderness serves as a model for us.

In the same way, when you feel the pangs of hunger, remember that God is inviting you to turn to His Word for nourishment. Let His promises, His truths, and His love fill the spaces where physical food once was. Trust that He will provide what you need, both spiritually and physically.

> **KEY THOUGHT:**
> **GOD'S PROVISION IS ABUNDANT AND COMPLETE.**

Today's key thought centers on the truth that God's provision is both abundant and complete. Fasting is a way of making room in your life for God's provision, trusting that He knows exactly what you need—even better than you do.

It's easy to rely on our own efforts and resources to meet our needs, but fasting reminds us that everything we have comes from God. He provides not only the food we eat but the air we breathe, the relationships we cherish, and the opportunities we receive. His provision is perfect, and it lacks nothing.

As you fast today, meditate on the completeness of God's provision. There is nothing you lack in Christ. Even in times of physical hunger, you can be satisfied knowing that God's love and grace are more than enough. Trust that He is meeting your needs, even the ones you may not be aware of.

> ## PRAYER PROMPT: **A PRAYER FOR TRUST**

Today's prayer focus is on trusting God as your provider. This is an opportunity to surrender any anxieties or doubts you have about whether God will meet your needs, and to place your full confidence in His care.

PRAYER PROMPT:

> *"Father, today I come to You, recognizing that You are my ultimate provider. I thank You for all the ways You have provided for me in the past, and I trust that You will continue to meet my needs, both during this fast and in every area of my life. Lord, I surrender any anxieties or fears I have about not having enough—whether that's food, finances, or even strength. I acknowledge that everything I need comes from You, and I choose to place my trust in Your perfect provision. Help me to lean into You during this fast, to rely on Your word for sustenance, and to trust that You will provide for my physical, emotional, and spiritual needs. Thank You for being a faithful provider, and for always giving me what I need. In Jesus's name, I pray. Amen."*

> ## SCIENTIFIC INSIGHT:
> ## KETOSIS AND INCREASED MENTAL CLARITY

KEYWORD DEFINITION: KETONES

Ketones are small molecules produced by your liver when your body switches to burning fat for fuel instead of carbohydrates. Imagine that your body usually relies on glucose (from carbs) for quick energy, but when glucose isn't available, such as during fasting or a low-carb diet, it taps into fat stores instead. The liver breaks down fat and produces ketones as a byproduct, which then circulate in your bloodstream to be used as energy, especially by the brain.

This shift to ketones is a natural and efficient process, providing a steady energy source that many find improves mental clarity and endurance.[6]

On Day 3, your body is beginning to adapt more fully to the fast. By now, your glycogen stores are nearly depleted, and your body is starting to rely on fat for energy. This process, known as ketosis, is in full swing.

As your body begins burning fat for fuel, it produces ketones—molecules that serve as an alternative energy source, especially for the brain. One of the interesting effects of this metabolic shift is increased mental clarity. Many people report feeling more focused and mentally sharp during a fast, particularly once their body has fully entered ketosis.

Ketones are a highly efficient fuel for the brain, and research has shown that they can enhance cognitive function, improve focus, and even provide neuroprotective benefits. This is why some people use intermittent fasting or ketogenic diets to boost brain performance.

While you may still experience moments of hunger, irritability, or fatigue as your body adjusts, there's also a growing sense of mental clarity that comes with fasting. Pay attention to how your mind feels today—are you able to focus more easily on prayer, meditation, or Scripture reading? This increased clarity is one of the hidden benefits of fasting, allowing you to connect more deeply with God as your mind becomes less cluttered.

---

6 John C. Newman and Eric Verdin, "Ketone bodies as signaling metabolites," *Trends in Endocrinology & Metabolism* 25, no. 1 (2014): 42-52, http://dx.doi.org/10.1016/j.tem.2013.09.002.

DAY 3 TIP:
HYDRATION SUPPORTS CLEANSING AND ENERGY

By Day 3, your body is in full adaptation mode, and staying hydrated is crucial for both energy and cleansing. As your body burns through stored resources, water helps flush out the byproducts and toxins being released, supporting a smoother detox process. Hydration also helps maintain mental clarity and reduces any lingering fatigue. Continue to drink regularly throughout the day; warm water or herbal tea can be particularly soothing if you're experiencing any digestive shifts. Remember, each sip is aiding your body in this stretch of the fast!

JOURNALING:
REFLECTING ON TRUST AND PROVISION

Journaling today is an opportunity to reflect on how God has provided for you in the past and how He is providing for you now, especially during this fast. Use this time to document your thoughts, prayers, and any insights you receive about trust and provision.

JOURNALING PROMPTS:

1) In what areas of your life do you struggle to trust God's provision? Write about any specific areas where you find it difficult to let go and trust God to meet your needs. What fears or doubts are preventing you from trusting Him fully?

_____

_____

2) How has God provided for you in the past? Reflect on specific instances where you have seen God's provision in your life, whether it's through finances, relationships, guidance, or other means. How does remembering these instances increase your faith in the future?

3) What does it mean for you to "live on every word that comes from the mouth of God"? Consider how God's word sustains you spiritually. How can you lean more on His word during this fast, especially when physical hunger arises?

4) How is your body responding to the fast on Day 3? Describe any physical sensations, emotions, or changes in mental clarity that you're experiencing. How are you adapting to this shift?

5) What prayers of trust are on your heart today? Write out a personal prayer asking God to help you trust Him more deeply in every area of your life. Express your gratitude for His provision and your faith that He will continue to provide for you.

Trust in God's Provision **57**

_____

_____

_____

_____

_____

Journaling helps you document your journey and gives you a space to see how God is working in your life, even in ways you may not realize immediately. As you write, allow yourself to be honest about the challenges of trusting God and celebrate the moments where you see His provision clearly.

ENCOURAGEMENT FOR THE JOURNEY AHEAD

As you conclude Day 3, take a moment to reflect on the truth that God is always faithful to provide. His provision is not limited by your circumstances, your resources, or your abilities. He is the God of abundance, and He knows exactly what you need before you even ask.

Today may have brought challenges—perhaps physical hunger, fatigue, or emotional struggles. But remember that God's grace is sufficient for you, and His provision is not just about meeting your physical needs. He is also providing peace, strength, and guidance as you continue this journey.

Trust is built over time, and fasting is one of the ways that God helps us to grow in our trust in Him. The more you surrender control and allow God to provide, the more you will experience His faithfulness in new and profound ways.

> ## LOOKING AHEAD: **PREPARING FOR DAY 4**

Tomorrow, as you move into Day 4, the focus will be on finding strength in weakness. Fasting is a humbling experience that often reveals our limitations, but it is in these moments of weakness that God's strength shines through most clearly.

As you prepare for tomorrow, ask God to give you the grace to embrace your weakness and trust in His strength to carry you through. Rest in the knowledge that His power is made perfect in your weakness, and look forward to experiencing His strength in new ways.

CHAPTER 5

DAY 4

STRENGTH IN WEAKNESS

EMBRACING YOUR WEAKNESS

Welcome to Day 4 of your fasting journey. By now, you've likely experienced the initial challenges of fasting: the hunger pangs, the physical fatigue, and perhaps even some emotional turbulence. These are natural parts of the fasting process, and they serve as reminders of our human limitations. Today's focus is on finding strength in those very limitations.

Fasting is a humbling experience. It brings you face-to-face with your own frailty and dependence. But rather than seeing weakness as a negative, today's journey invites you to see it as a gateway to experiencing God's strength in a profound way. When we come to the end of our own strength, we make room for God's power to work in us more fully.

Today is about learning to embrace your weakness, not as a defeat, but as an opportunity to lean on God more deeply. In your moments of physical and emotional vulnerability, God's strength is there to sustain you and carry you through.

OVERVIEW OF DAY 4: FINDING GOD'S STRENGTH IN YOUR WEAKNESS

The theme for Day 4 is strength in weakness. This concept may seem counterintuitive, especially in a world that values self-reliance and strength. However, the Bible teaches us that true strength is found not in our own abilities, but in our dependence on God.

As you progress through your fast, you might feel weaker physically, and that's okay. These moments of weakness are invitations to turn to God, who promises to be your strength. Today is about shifting your focus from what you can do on your own to what God can do in and through you when you surrender to Him.

When you embrace your weakness, you're not giving up; you're opening yourself up to God's power. Fasting brings this truth into sharp focus, revealing that our real strength comes not from our physical condition but from our connection to God.

SCRIPTURE OF THE DAY: 2 CORINTHIANS 12:9-10

But he said to me, "My grace is sufficient for you, for my power is made perfect in weakness." Therefore I will boast all the more gladly of my weaknesses, so that the power of Christ may rest upon me. For the sake of Christ, then, I am content with weaknesses, insults, hardships, persecutions, and calamities. For when I am weak, then I am strong. —2 Corinthians 12:9-10 (ESV)

In today's scripture, the Apostle Paul shares a profound truth: that God's power is made perfect in our weakness. Paul had pleaded with God to remove a "thorn in the flesh," but God's response was not to remove the difficulty but to provide grace to endure it. This passage teaches us that God's grace is not just sufficient; it is abundant and powerful enough to turn our weaknesses into strengths.

As you meditate on this scripture today, consider how God is using your fasting journey to reveal His strength in your life. Your physical weakness—whether it's hunger, fatigue, or discomfort—can become a platform for God's power to be displayed. Instead of focusing on your limitations, focus on the sufficiency of God's grace.

> **KEY THOUGHT:**
> **GOD'S POWER IS PERFECTED IN WEAKNESS.**

Today's key thought is that God's power is perfected in weakness. This is a central theme in the Christian life and one that fasting uniquely highlights. When you are at your weakest, God is able to work most powerfully, because it is then that you are most reliant on Him.

Our culture often teaches us to hide or overcome our weaknesses, but the Bible encourages us to embrace them because it is through our weaknesses that God's strength is made visible. Fasting strips away our illusions of self-sufficiency and reveals our deep need for God's grace and power.

As you move through today, remember that your weakness is not something to be ashamed of; it is an opportunity for God's power to be manifested in your life. When you feel weary, discouraged, or overwhelmed, take comfort in knowing that God's grace is sufficient for you and that His power is at work in your life.

> ## PRAYER PROMPT:
> ## A PRAYER FOR STRENGTH IN WEAKNESS

Today's prayer focus is on asking God for strength in your moments of weakness. This is an opportunity to invite God's power into the areas where you feel most vulnerable and to trust that He will sustain you.

PRAYER PROMPT:

"Lord, I come to You today acknowledging my weakness. I confess that I often try to rely on my own strength, but I know that true strength comes from You alone. I thank You for the reminder that Your grace is sufficient for me and that Your power is made perfect in my weakness. I surrender my fatigue, my hunger, and any feelings of discouragement to You, and I ask that You fill me with Your strength. Help me to lean on You more fully, to trust in Your power, and to rest in the knowledge that You are with me. Thank You for turning my weakness into an opportunity for Your strength to be displayed. I place my trust in You, knowing that when I am weak, You are strong. In Jesus's name, I pray. Amen."

> ## SCIENTIFIC INSIGHT: THE BODY'S ADAPTATION AND SUSTAINED ENERGY

KEYWORD DEFINITION: GLYCOGEN

Glycogen is your body's stored form of glucose, which is the primary fuel it uses for quick energy. Think of glycogen as your energy reserve tank—it's stored in your liver and muscles and can be quickly converted back into glucose when your body needs a burst of energy. During fasting or prolonged exercise, your body starts to tap into these glycogen stores to keep your blood sugar steady and provide fuel, especially in the early stages, before switching to fat as a primary energy source.[7]

By Day 4, your body is adapting more fully to the fasting state. The initial discomforts of hunger and fatigue may still be present, but your body is becoming more efficient at using its stored energy. This is a critical phase where your body transitions from relying primarily on glycogen (stored glucose) to using fat as its primary fuel source.

As your body continues to produce ketones, these molecules provide a steady and sustained source of energy, particularly for your brain. While fasting, your body is also prioritizing energy for essential functions, which means you may notice a reduction in non-essential activities like digestion. This shift allows your body to conserve energy and focus on internal healing and repair.

One of the significant benefits of this adaptation is increased energy efficiency. Although you might feel physically weaker, your body is working in a highly efficient mode, using its resources more effectively. This can lead to improved mental clarity, a sense of calm, and a deeper awareness of your body's capabilities.

It's important to listen to your body during this time. While fasting is beneficial, it's also a time to be gentle with yourself. If you feel tired, rest. If you experience dizziness or discomfort, take a moment to breathe and hydrate. Your body is undergoing a significant adjustment, and it's crucial to support it through rest, prayer, and hydration.

---

7 Frans Huijin, "Glycogen Metabolism and Glycogen-Storage Diseases," *Physiological Reviews* 55, no. 4 (1975): 609-58, https://doi.org/10.1152/physrev.1975.55.4.609.

DAY 4 TIP:
HYDRATION FOR TRANSITION AND BALANCE

On Day 4 of your twenty-one-day fast, your body is entering a deeper phase of transition, relying more on stored energy. Drinking water is essential at this stage to help balance this shift, as it keeps your system hydrated and supports the elimination of toxins. Staying hydrated can also prevent lightheadedness or fatigue that may arise as your body adapts. Make a habit of sipping water regularly throughout the day—adding a slice of lemon can add a bit of flavor and further assist the detox process. Your hydration is key to sustaining balance as you continue on this journey!

JOURNALING:
REFLECTING ON STRENGTH AND WEAKNESS

Journaling today is an opportunity to reflect on the relationship between your weakness and God's strength. Use this time to document your thoughts, emotions, and any insights you receive about how God is working in your life through your fasting journey.

JOURNALING PROMPTS:

1) In what areas of your life do you feel weak or vulnerable right now? Write about any physical, emotional, or spiritual weaknesses you're experiencing. How are these weaknesses affecting you, and how are you responding to them?

_____

_____

2) How has God's strength been evident in your life during this fast? Reflect on specific instances where you've felt God's presence, guidance, or support. How has He provided strength in your moments of weakness?

3) What does it mean to you that God's power is made perfect in your weakness? Consider how this truth applies to your current situation. How can you embrace your weakness as an opportunity for God's power to be displayed?

4) How is your body adapting to the fast on Day 4? Describe any changes you're noticing in your physical energy, mental clarity, or emotional state. How are you supporting your body through this adaptation?

5) What prayers of strength are on your heart today? Write out a personal prayer asking God to continue providing strength in your areas of weakness. Express your gratitude for His grace and power.

_____

_____

_____

_____

_____

_____

_____

Journaling helps you to process the deep work God is doing in your heart during this time. It's a way to capture the spiritual insights and personal growth that fasting facilitates, and it serves as a reminder of God's faithfulness in your life.

ENCOURAGEMENT FOR THE JOURNEY AHEAD

As you conclude Day 4, take comfort in the truth that God's strength is with you, even when you feel weak. Fasting is a journey that reveals our limitations, but it also reveals God's unlimited power and grace. When you feel tired, when you're tempted to give up, remember that God's strength is made perfect in your weakness.

The journey of fasting is not just about going without food; it's about discovering the depths of God's provision, grace, and power in your life. Each day is an opportunity to lean more fully on Him, experience His sustaining power, and grow in your faith.

As you continue, keep your focus on God. Let Him be your source of strength, your refuge, and your guide. He is with you, and He will carry you through each moment of this journey.

> ## LOOKING AHEAD: **PREPARING FOR DAY 5**

Tomorrow, as you move into Day 5, the focus will be on the power of prayer. Prayer is a vital part of fasting, and it is through prayer that we connect most deeply with God. On Day 5, you'll explore how fasting enhances the power of your prayers and how to use this time to intercede for yourself, your loved ones, and the world around you.

As you prepare for tomorrow, spend some time tonight in quiet reflection. Ask God to prepare your heart for a deeper encounter with Him through prayer. Trust that He is already at work, shaping your heart and mind for the days ahead.

CHAPTER 6

DAY 5

THE POWER OF PRAYER

DEEPENING YOUR CONNECTION WITH GOD

Welcome to Day 5 of your fasting journey. By now, you've likely settled into the rhythm of your fast, and while the physical challenges may still be present, today invites you to shift your focus even more deeply toward the spiritual. Today's theme is the power of prayer, a vital element that not only sustains you during fasting but also amplifies the spiritual impact of your fast.

Prayer is the heartbeat of fasting. Without it, fasting is merely an act of physical deprivation. But with prayer, fasting becomes a powerful tool for spiritual growth, breakthrough, and intimacy with God. On this fifth day, you're encouraged to lean into prayer like never before, allowing it to fuel your spirit and guide you through this journey.

This chapter will help you explore how fasting intensifies prayer, how to pray effectively during a fast, and how to harness the power of prayer to align your heart with God's will.

OVERVIEW OF DAY 5: UNLEASHING THE POWER OF PRAYER

The theme for Day 5 is centered on the transformative power of prayer, especially in the context of fasting. When you fast, your prayers are more focused, more fervent, and often more powerful. Fasting strips away distractions, enabling you to connect with God on a deeper level and to pray with greater clarity and intention.

Throughout the Bible, we see that fasting and prayer often go hand in hand. Whether it's Daniel seeking wisdom, Esther interceding for her people, or Jesus preparing for His ministry, fasting amplifies the power of prayer. It creates a spiritual environment where you are more attuned to God's voice and more aligned with His purposes.

Today, you're invited to deepen your prayer life, bring your needs, desires, and struggles before God, and listen closely for His guidance. Prayer is not just about speaking to God; it's about listening to Him, receiving His wisdom, and aligning your will with His.

SCRIPTURE OF THE DAY: JAMES 5:16

"The prayer of a righteous person is powerful and effective."—James 5:16

Today's scripture from the book of James highlights the incredible power of prayer. James reminds us that the prayers of a righteous person—someone who is in right standing with God—are not just heard by God; they are powerful and effective. This means that your prayers, especially when coupled with fasting, have the ability to bring about real change.

As you meditate on this verse, consider the areas of your life where you need to see God's power at work. What situations, relationships, or challenges are you facing that require divine intervention? Fasting amplifies the effectiveness of your prayers, creating a spiritual environment where God's power can move mightily.

Remember, it's not about the eloquence of your words or the length of your prayers; it's about the sincerity of your heart and your alignment with God's will. Today, focus on praying with faith, knowing that God hears you and that your prayers are powerful and effective.

> **KEY THOUGHT:**
> **FASTING AMPLIFIES THE POWER OF PRAYER.**

Today's key thought is that fasting amplifies the power of prayer. When you fast, you're not just abstaining from food; you're making room for God to work more fully in your life. This creates a fertile ground for your prayers to take root and bear fruit.

Throughout the Bible, fasting is often linked with intense prayer. In the book of Daniel, for example, Daniel fasted and prayed for twenty-one days, seeking understanding and guidance from God (Daniel 10). His fasting amplified his prayers, leading to a powerful vision and a divine response.

Fasting helps to purify your motives, clarify your desires, and align your heart with God's will. When you fast and pray, you're not just asking God to do something for you; you're positioning yourself to receive from Him and to be used by Him in powerful ways. As you pray today, remember that your fasting is strengthening your prayers, making them more focused, more fervent, and more aligned with God's purposes.

> ### PRAYER PROMPT:
> ### A PRAYER FOR EMPOWERED INTERCESSION

Today's prayer focus is on intercession—praying not just for your own needs but for the needs of others, your community, and the world. This is an opportunity to harness the power of fasting to pray effectively for those around you, knowing that your prayers are making a difference.

PRAYER PROMPT:

"Father, I come to You today with a heart full of gratitude and expectation. I thank You for the gift of prayer, and for the privilege of coming before You with my needs and the needs of others. Lord, I ask that You empower my prayers today, that they would be aligned with Your will and filled with faith. I lift up the needs of my loved ones, my community, and the world. I pray for Your healing, provision, and guidance to be poured out. I ask for wisdom and discernment as I intercede for those who are hurting, lost, or in need of Your touch. Help me to pray with boldness and confidence, knowing that my prayers are powerful and effective because of Your grace. Thank You for hearing my prayers and for moving in ways that I cannot see. I trust you, Lord, and I give You all the glory. In Jesus's name, I pray. Amen."

> ### SCIENTIFIC INSIGHT: STABILIZATION OF KETOSIS

KEYWORD DEFINITION: PREFRONTAL CORTEX

The prefrontal cortex is the part of your brain that sits right behind your forehead and acts as the "executive" center, responsible for decision-making, planning, and self-control. It's the area that helps you think things through, manage impulses, and make considered choices. During fasting, the prefrontal cortex plays a crucial role in regulating behavior, helping you resist cravings and stay focused on your goals. This part of the brain is involved in some of our most complex behaviors, which is why keeping it healthy and functioning optimally is key to making good decisions and maintaining self-discipline.[8]

Today, you're likely feeling more stable. Your body is getting better at producing and using ketones, which means your energy levels should be evening out. Hunger pangs are probably fading, and you're hitting a rhythm in your fast.

The Impact of Prayer on the Brain

Remember, prayer is not only a spiritual practice; it also has profound effects on the brain. Neuroscientific research has shown that engaging in regular prayer can bring about significant changes in brain structure and function, which can enhance mental and emotional well-being.[9]

Activation of the Prefrontal Cortex

One of the key areas affected by prayer is the prefrontal cortex, the region of the brain associated with decision-making, focus, and self-control. During prayer, the prefrontal cortex is activated, leading to improved concentration and the ability to regulate emotions more effectively. This activation is particularly beneficial during fasting, as it can help you maintain focus on your spiritual goals and resist the physical discomforts of fasting.

Dr. Andrew Newberg, a leading neuroscientist in the field of neurotheology, professor, and Director of Research at Jefferson Health Marcus Institute of Integrative Health, has conducted extensive research on how spiritual practices like prayer and meditation affect the brain. In his book, *How God Changes*

---

[8] William R. Hathaway and Bruce W. Newton, "Neuroanatomy, Prefrontal Cortex," (2018).
[9] Dr. Andrew Newberg and Mark Robert Waldman, *How God Changes Your Brain: Breakthrough Findings from a Leading Neuroscientist* (New York, NY: Ballantine Books, 2009).

Your Brain, Newberg explains that prayer can increase activity in the prefrontal cortex, leading to better cognitive function and emotional stability.[10]

Enhanced Effects During Fasting

When combined with fasting, the effects of prayer on the brain can be even more profound. Fasting often leads to increased mental clarity and spiritual sensitivity, which enhances the depth and intensity of prayer. As your body enters a state of ketosis, your brain becomes more efficient at using ketones for energy, resulting in sustained mental clarity and focus. This makes your prayer time more fruitful and your connection with God more profound.

In summary, prayer is not only a spiritual discipline but also a practice that can positively influence your brain's function, enhancing your mental clarity, emotional regulation, and overall well-being during fasting. The combined effects of fasting and prayer can lead to profound spiritual and neurological benefits, helping you to connect more deeply with God and experience His presence in powerful ways.

> **DAY 5 TIP:**
> **WATER KEEPS YOU ENERGIZED AND CLEAR**

By Day 5 of your twenty-one-day fast, staying hydrated is essential for maintaining steady energy and mental clarity. Drinking water helps your body efficiently burn fat and flush out waste products as it adapts to fasting. You may notice that regular hydration reduces feelings of sluggishness and even helps keep your mood balanced. Try to keep a water bottle with you and sip throughout the day—staying hydrated will support both your physical and mental resilience as you continue your journey. Adding a pinch of sea salt can also help replenish electrolytes naturally if you're feeling low on energy.

---

[10] Newberg and Waldman, *How God Changes Your Brain.*

JOURNALING: REFLECTING ON THE POWER OF PRAYER

Journaling today provides an opportunity to reflect on the role of prayer in your fasting journey. Use this time to document your thoughts, prayers, and any insights you receive about how God is moving in your life through prayer.

JOURNALING PROMPTS:

1) How has your prayer life been impacted by fasting so far? Reflect on any changes you've noticed in your prayer habits, focus, or effectiveness since you began fasting. How has fasting deepened your connection with God through prayer?

_____

_____

_____

_____

_____

_____

_____

2) What specific prayers are you bringing before God today? Write down the people, situations, and needs that you're praying for. How are you trusting God to move in these areas?

_____

_____

3) How have you seen the power of prayer at work in your life? Consider past experiences where you've seen God answer prayers in powerful ways. How does this encourage you to pray with greater faith today?

4) How are your body and mind responding to the combination of fasting and prayer? Describe any physical sensations, mental clarity, or emotional shifts you're experiencing as you engage more deeply in prayer during this fast.

5) What prayers of intercession are on your heart today? Write out a personal prayer for the needs of others, your community, and the world. Use this space to intercede with boldness, trusting that God hears and responds to your prayers.

Journaling helps you to capture the spiritual work that God is doing in your life during this fast. It's a way to document your journey, celebrate answered prayers, and reflect on how prayer and fasting are transforming you from the inside out.

ENCOURAGEMENT FOR THE JOURNEY AHEAD

As you conclude Day 5, take comfort in the truth that your prayers are powerful and effective. Fasting has brought you to a place of greater spiritual sensitivity, where your prayers are not only heard by God but are also moving heaven and earth. This is the power of prayer amplified by fasting.

Remember that prayer is both a privilege and a responsibility. It's a way to connect with God, seek His will, and partner with Him in bringing about His purposes on earth. As you continue to fast, let prayer be the fuel that sustains you, guides you, and empowers you to walk in God's will.

Each day of your fasting journey brings you closer to God and deeper into His presence. As you pray, know that you are not just speaking into the void; you are engaging with the Creator of the universe, who delights in hearing your voice and responding to your needs.

LOOKING AHEAD: **PREPARING FOR DAY 6**

Tomorrow, as you move into Day 6, the focus will be on embracing the spiritual journey of fasting. By now, you've begun to experience the depth of what fasting can do, not just physically but spiritually. On Day 6, you'll delve deeper into understanding the spiritual significance of your fast, recognizing the ways God is working in and through you as you continue this transformative journey.

CHAPTER 7

DAY 6

EMBRACING THE SPIRITUAL JOURNEY

JOURNEYING DEEPER WITH GOD

Welcome to Day 6 of your fasting journey. By now, you've likely begun to experience the deepening spiritual impact of your fast. Fasting is more than just abstaining from food; it's about embarking on a spiritual journey that brings you closer to God, helps you gain clarity, and fosters personal transformation. Today's focus is on fully embracing this spiritual journey, recognizing the profound work God is doing in and through you as you continue to fast.

As you move further into your fast, the physical discomforts may still be present, but they are often accompanied by a greater sense of spiritual awareness and sensitivity. This is a sign that you're entering deeper into the spiritual aspects of fasting, where God's presence becomes more tangible, and His voice clearer.

Today's chapter will guide you through understanding the spiritual significance of your fast, how to lean into the process, and how to embrace the changes God is bringing about in your life.

> **OVERVIEW OF DAY 6:**
> **EMBRACING TRANSFORMATION**

The theme for Day 6 is embracing the spiritual journey of fasting. Fasting is a process that involves stripping away the physical to reveal and refine the spiritual. It's a journey that requires patience, surrender, and trust in God's work in your life. As you fast, you're not just abstaining from food; you're creating space for God to move in powerful ways.

The journey of fasting is often compared to a refining fire—a process that purifies and strengthens. As you continue to fast, you may notice areas of your life that God is refining, whether it's your thoughts, habits, or relationships. This is a time to embrace the work He is doing, even if it's uncomfortable or challenging.

Today is about surrendering fully to the journey, trusting that God is using this fast to transform you into the person He created you to be. As you embrace the spiritual journey, you'll begin to see the fruits of your fasting, both in your relationship with God and in the way you live your life.

> **SCRIPTURE OF THE DAY: ROMANS 12:2**

Do not conform to the pattern of this world, but be transformed by the renewing of your mind. Then you will be able to test and approve what God's will is—his good, pleasing and perfect will. —Romans 12:2

Today's scripture from Romans encourages you to embrace transformation through the renewal of your mind. Fasting is a powerful tool for this kind of transformation, as it helps to break the patterns of the world and align your thoughts and actions with God's will.

As you meditate on this verse, consider how your fast is renewing your mind. Are there thoughts, behaviors, or attitudes that God is challenging you to change? How is He using this time of fasting to transform you from the inside out?

Transformation is not just about behavior modification; it's about deep, spiritual change that aligns your heart and mind with God's purposes. As you continue your fast today, invite God to renew your mind, break any patterns that are not in line with His will, and transform you into the person He has called you to be.

> **KEY THOUGHT:**
> **FASTING IS A JOURNEY OF TRANSFORMATION.**

Today's key thought is that fasting is a journey of transformation. The physical aspects of fasting—such as hunger and fatigue—are often the most noticeable, but the real work happens on a spiritual level. Fasting is a process that refines your character, deepens your faith, and aligns your life with God's will.

Transformation through fasting is not always immediate or dramatic. Often, it's a slow and steady process, where God works on your heart and mind day by day. This transformation is about becoming more like Christ, shedding the old self, and embracing the new.

As you reflect on your journey so far, think about the areas where you've already seen God at work. How has He been transforming your thoughts, your desires, or your relationships? Embrace this process, knowing that God is faithful to complete the work He has begun in you (Philippians 1:6).

> **PRAYER PROMPT:**
> **A PRAYER FOR TRANSFORMATION**

Today's prayer focus is on asking God to continue His work of transformation in your life. This is an opportunity to surrender any areas that need refining and to invite God to renew your mind and heart.

PRAYER PROMPT:

"Lord, I come to You today, grateful for the work You are doing in my life through this fast. I recognize that fasting is not just about physical discipline but about spiritual transformation. I ask that You continue to renew my mind and align my thoughts and desires with Your will. Help me to see the areas of my life that need to change, and give me the courage to surrender them to You. Lord, I want to be transformed into the person You have created me to be—someone who reflects Your love, grace, and truth. Thank You for the work You are doing in me, even when I can't see it. I trust that You are faithful to complete this work, and I surrender fully to Your process. In Jesus's name, I pray. Amen."

> **SCIENTIFIC INSIGHT:**
> **CELLULAR REGENERATION BEGINS**

KEYWORD DEFINITION: NEUROPLASTICITY

Neuroplasticity is your brain's amazing ability to reorganize and adapt by forming new connections between neurons (brain cells). Think of it like rewiring a circuit board: when you learn something new, practice a skill, or change a habit, your brain creates new pathways and strengthens existing ones. During fasting, certain processes in the brain may enhance neuroplasticity, which can support improved focus, mental clarity, and learning abilities. Neuroplasticity is a vital part of how we adapt to new experiences, overcome challenges, and even recover from injuries to the brain.[11]

You're entering a phase where deep cellular repair is happening. Autophagy continues its work, and growth hormone levels are rising, which helps preserve muscle and boosts fat metabolism. You might feel minor fatigue, but overall, your body is starting to rejuvenate.

NEUROPLASTICITY AND SPIRITUAL TRANSFORMATION

The concept of transformation is not only spiritual but also supported by scientific understanding of the brain's ability to change and adapt—a phenomenon known as neuroplasticity. Neuroplasticity refers to the brain's capacity to reorganize itself by forming new neural connections throughout life. This ability is crucial for learning, memory, and adapting to new experiences, including spiritual practices like fasting and prayer.

The Role of Neuroplasticity in Spiritual Practices

Neuroplasticity is a key factor in how spiritual practices, such as fasting and prayer, can lead to lasting transformation. When you engage in these practices, you are not only strengthening your spiritual life but also reshaping your brain. According to Dr. Richard Davidson, a neuroscientist and psychologist, regular spiritual practices can lead to changes in brain structure and function, particularly in areas related to attention, emotion regulation, and compassion.[12]

During fasting, your brain is more receptive to these changes due to increased focus and reduced distractions. As you pray and meditate on God's Word, you are reinforcing neural pathways that support positive spiritual

---
11 Giorgio M. Innocenti, "Chapter 1 – Defining Neuroplasticity," *Handbook of Clinical Neurology* 184 (2022): 3-18, https://doi.org/10.1016/B978-0-12-819410-2.00001-1.
12 Daniel Coleman and Richard J. Davidson, *Altered Traits: Science Reveals How Meditation Changes Your Mind, Brain, and Body* (New York, NY: Penguin, 2018).

habits and behaviors. Over time, these repeated practices lead to lasting changes in your brain, making it easier to maintain a life aligned with God's will.

DAY 6 TIP:
HYDRATION SUPPORTS DETOX AND VITALITY

On Day 6 of your twenty-one-day fast, your body is in a deeper state of detoxification and energy shift. Drinking water is crucial to support this process, as it aids in flushing out the byproducts of stored fat and other energy sources your body is now using. Staying well-hydrated also keeps your energy steady and helps prevent any potential dizziness or fatigue as your metabolism continues to adjust. Aim to drink water regularly throughout the day—consider herbal teas or adding a few cucumber slices for variety. Hydration will keep you feeling refreshed and clear-headed as you progress in your fast!

JOURNALING:
REFLECTING ON TRANSFORMATION

Journaling today provides an opportunity to reflect on the transformative journey of your fast. Use this time to document your thoughts, prayers, and any insights you receive about how God is working in your life through this process.

JOURNALING PROMPTS:

1) How have you experienced transformation during this fast so far? Reflect on any changes you've noticed in your thoughts, behaviors, or spiritual life. How is God using this fast to refine and renew you?

---

2) What areas of your life do you feel God is still working on? Write down any specific areas where you sense God is leading you to change or grow. How are you responding to His work in these areas?

3) How does the concept of neuroplasticity enhance your understanding of spiritual transformation? Consider how the brain's ability to change supports the idea of renewing the mind. How does this scientific insight encourage you in your spiritual journey?

THE **FASTING** Companion

_____
_____
_____
_____
_____
_____

4) What prayers of transformation are on your heart today? Write out a personal prayer asking God to continue His work of transformation in your life. Express your willingness to be molded and shaped according to His will.

_____
_____
_____
_____
_____
_____
_____

Journaling helps you to capture the spiritual work that God is doing in your life during this fast. It's a way to document your journey, celebrate the transformation you're experiencing, and reflect on how fasting is shaping you into the person God has called you to be.

ENCOURAGEMENT FOR THE JOURNEY AHEAD

As you conclude Day 6, take a moment to reflect on the transformation that is occurring in your life. Fasting is a powerful tool that God uses to refine, renew, and transform you from the inside out. While the process may not always be easy, it is producing lasting change that aligns your heart and mind with God's purposes.

Remember that transformation is a journey, not a destination. Each day of your fast brings you closer to the person God

CHAPTER 8

DAY 7

RESTING IN GOD'S PRESENCE

THE GIFT OF REST

Welcome to Day 7 of your fasting journey. You've completed the first week, a significant milestone in this spiritual adventure. By now, you've likely experienced both the challenges and the rewards of fasting moments of weakness, clarity, and spiritual insight. Today's focus is on resting in God's presence, an essential aspect of your fast that allows you to recharge spiritually, mentally, and physically.

Rest is a gift from God, a vital component of a healthy spiritual life. In our busy world, it's easy to overlook the importance of rest, but fasting teaches us the value of slowing down, quieting our minds, and allowing God to refresh us. Today, you're invited to embrace this gift, cease striving, and simply be still in God's presence.

This chapter will guide you in understanding the importance of rest during fasting, how to enter into God's rest, and the benefits of allowing your body and spirit to recharge during this time.

OVERVIEW OF DAY 7: EMBRACING REST

The theme for Day 7 is resting in God's presence. Fasting is not just about abstaining from food or seeking spiritual breakthroughs; it's also about learning to rest in the assurance of God's love and provision. Rest is a critical part of your fasting journey because it allows your body to heal, your mind to clear, and your spirit to connect more deeply with God.

Rest is often misunderstood as inactivity, but true rest is an active surrender to God, trusting Him to work in you and through you as you cease from your own efforts. As you fast, your body is already doing a significant amount of work—detoxifying, healing, and adapting. Spiritual rest mirrors this physical process, where you let go of your striving and allow God to do His work in you.

Today is about intentionally slowing down, turning off distractions, and spending time in quiet reflection and prayer. It's a day to embrace stillness, listen for God's voice, and allow His peace to fill your heart and mind.

SCRIPTURE OF THE DAY: PSALM 46:10

"Be still, and know that I am God; I will be exalted among the nations, I will be exalted in the earth."—Psalm 46:10

Today's scripture from Psalm 46:10 is a powerful reminder of the importance of being still and recognizing God's sovereignty. In the midst of life's chaos and challenges, God invites us to be still, cease our striving, and acknowledge His power and presence.

As you meditate on this verse, consider what it means to be still before God. In what areas of your life are you striving or trying to control outcomes? How can you surrender these areas to God and rest in His presence?

Resting in God's presence is not just about physical rest but also about spiritual surrender. It's about trusting that God is in control, that He is working on your behalf, and that He will be exalted in every situation. Today, let this verse guide you into a place of stillness, where you can experience the peace and assurance that comes from knowing God is with you.

> **KEY THOUGHT: RESTING IS TRUSTING**

Today's key thought is that resting in God's presence is an act of trust. When you rest, you're acknowledging that God is in control and that you don't have to carry the weight of the world on your shoulders. Fasting, combined with rest, deepens this trust as you let go of your own efforts and rely on God's strength.

Rest is a form of worship. It's a way of saying, "Lord, I trust You enough to stop my striving and simply be in Your presence." This rest is not passive; it's an active choice to surrender your worries, fears, and burdens to God. It's about finding peace in the knowledge that God is working even when you're not.

As you move through today, focus on the areas where you need to trust God more. Use this time of rest to deepen your reliance on Him, knowing that true rest comes from trusting in His provision and care.

> **PRAYER PROMPT: A PRAYER FOR REST**

Today's prayer focus is on asking God to help you enter into His rest. This is an opportunity to lay down your burdens, cease from striving, and find peace in God's presence.

PRAYER PROMPT:

"Father, I come to You today with a heart that longs for Your rest. I recognize that I often strive and struggle in my own strength, but today I choose to surrender to You. Help me to be still and know that You are God, to trust that You are in control, and to find peace in Your presence. Lord, I lay down my worries, my fears, and my need to control, and I rest in the assurance of Your love and care. Thank You for being my refuge and strength, my ever-present help in times of trouble. As I rest in You today, renew my spirit, refresh my mind, and restore my body. In Jesus's name, I pray. Amen."

> ## SCIENTIFIC INSIGHT:
> ## INCREASED ENERGY AND MENTAL FOCUS

KEYWORD DEFINITION: REST

Rest is more than just taking a break; it's the body's essential recovery mode, allowing your mind and muscles to recharge, repair, and rebalance. During rest, many behind-the-scenes processes are at work: your muscles repair, your immune system strengthens, and your brain consolidates memories. In fasting, rest becomes even more critical, as it allows the body to focus its energy on internal repair processes rather than digestion. Resting helps you maintain mental clarity, emotional balance, and physical health, making it a key part of any healing or renewal process.[13]

By now, your body is pretty efficient at this fasting protocol. You're likely noticing a steady flow of energy and a sharpness in your thinking. Inflammation is decreasing, and your body is feeling lighter and more in tune with itself.

---

[13] James M. Krueger et al., "Brain organization and sleep function," *Behavioural Brain Research* 69, no.1-2 (1995): 177-85, https://doi.org/10.1016/0166-4328(95)00015-L.

THE NEUROSCIENCE OF REST AND RECOVERY

Rest is not only a spiritual practice but also a crucial component of brain health and overall well-being. Neuroscientific research has shown that rest plays a vital role in the brain's ability to recover, process information, and maintain cognitive function.

The Role of Rest in Brain Health

Rest allows the brain to enter a state of recovery, where it can repair itself and consolidate memories. During periods of rest, particularly deep rest or sleep, the brain clears out metabolic waste products, including beta-amyloid, a protein associated with Alzheimer's disease. This cleaning process is facilitated by the glymphatic system, a network of channels in the brain that becomes more active during rest and sleep. This was highlighted in a study published in *Cerebral Circulation – Cognition and Behavior,* which found that the brain's waste clearance is significantly enhanced during sleep and rest, underscoring the importance of rest for long-term brain health.[14]

The Impact of Rest on Emotional Regulation

Rest also plays a crucial role in emotional regulation. During rest, particularly during deep relaxation or meditation, the brain's parasympathetic nervous system is activated. This system is responsible for the body's "rest and digest" functions, which counteract the "fight or flight" responses governed by the sympathetic nervous system. When the parasympathetic system is activated, the brain and body experience a reduction in stress hormones like cortisol, leading to a state of calm and relaxation. This was supported by research published in *AIMS Neuroscience* which found that rest and mindfulness practices significantly reduce stress and improve emotional regulation.[15]

---

14 Keith A. Wafford, "Abberant waste disposal in neurodegeneration: Why improved sleep could be the solution," *Cerebral Circulation-Cognition and Behavior* 2 (2021): 100025, https://doi.org/10.1016/j.cccb.2021.100025.
15 Marie Vandekerckhove and Yu-lin Wang, "Emotion, emotion regulation and sleep: An intimate relationship," *AIMS Neuroscience* 5, no. 1 (2017): 1-17, https://doi.org/10.3934/Neuroscience.2018.1.1.

Rest and Fasting: A Powerful Combination

When combined with fasting, the benefits of rest can be even more pronounced. Fasting, while physically demanding, also encourages the body to enter a state of repair and renewal. Resting during a fast allows the body to focus its energy on these processes, enhancing the detoxification and healing effects of fasting.

Additionally, resting in God's presence during a fast can lead to deeper spiritual insights and a stronger connection with God. The combination of fasting and rest creates a space for God to work in your life, free from the distractions and busyness of daily life. This is supported by research on mindfulness and fasting practices, which shows that periods of rest and reflection during fasting can lead to enhanced spiritual and emotional well-being.

> **DAY 7 TIP: WATER FOR CELLULAR CLEANSING AND REJUVENATION**

On Day 7 of your twenty-one-day fast, your body is working hard at a cellular level to repair and rejuvenate. Drinking water is vital today, as it supports your cells in eliminating waste and staying hydrated for efficient functioning. Proper hydration also enhances mental clarity and helps prevent any lingering sluggishness or brain fog as your body adjusts further into the fast. Try to make water a steady companion throughout your day—adding a hint of lemon or a few mint leaves can add freshness. Remember, each sip is contributing to your body's deep cleansing and renewal!

JOURNALING: **REFLECTING ON REST**

Journaling today provides an opportunity to reflect on the importance of rest in your fasting journey. Use this time to document your thoughts, prayers, and any insights you receive about how rest is impacting your spiritual and physical well-being.

JOURNALING PROMPTS:

1) How have you experienced rest during this fast? Reflect on any moments of rest you've had, whether physical, mental, or spiritual. How has rest affected your fasting experience so far?

_____

_____

_____

_____

_____

_____

_____

_____

2) In what areas of your life do you need to trust God more? Write down any specific areas where you feel the need to strive or control. How can you surrender these areas to God and find rest in His presence?

_____

_____

3) How does the scientific understanding of rest enhance your appreciation for spiritual rest? Consider how the brain's need for rest aligns with the spiritual practice of resting in God. How does this insight encourage you to prioritize rest in your life?

4) What prayers of rest and surrender are on your heart today? Write out a personal prayer asking God to help you rest in His presence and trust in His provision. Express your desire to cease striving and to find peace in His care.

_____

_____

_____

_____

_____

_____

Journaling helps you to capture the spiritual and physical benefits of rest during your fast. It's a way to document your journey, reflect on the importance of rest, and deepen your connection with God.

ENCOURAGEMENT FOR THE JOURNEY AHEAD

As you conclude Day 7, take a moment to rest in the assurance of God's love and care for you. Fasting is a journey that requires both effort and rest, and today is an invitation to embrace the balance between the two. Remember that rest is not a luxury but a necessity, both for your body and your spirit.

Resting in God's presence is an act of trust, a way of acknowledging that He is in control and that you can cease from your own efforts. As you continue your fast, make rest a priority, knowing that it is through rest that God renews your strength, restores your soul, and deepens your relationship with Him.

Each day of your fasting journey brings you closer to God and deeper into His presence. As you rest today, know that you are not just pausing from activity; you are actively trusting in God's provision and care, allowing Him to work in and through you in powerful ways.

> ## LOOKING AHEAD: **PREPARING FOR WEEK 2**

Tomorrow marks the beginning of Week 2 of your fast. As you prepare for the days ahead, take time tonight to reflect on the first week and thank God for the work He has done in your life so far. Week 2 will focus on perseverance and deepening your spiritual insights, building on the foundation you've laid in the first week.

As you rest tonight, ask God to prepare your heart and mind for the next phase of your journey. Trust that He is with you, guiding you, and providing for you every step of the way.

CHAPTER 9

DAY 8

PERSEVERING THROUGH CHALLENGES

EMBRACING PERSEVERANCE

Welcome to Day 8 of your fasting journey. You've entered the second week of your fast, a crucial phase where perseverance becomes essential. The initial excitement and motivation that may have fueled the first few days are now being tested by the physical and mental challenges of prolonged fasting. Today's focus is on embracing perseverance, a vital quality that will carry you through the remaining days of your fast.

Perseverance is more than just enduring; it's about maintaining your commitment and focus despite difficulties. In fasting, perseverance involves pressing through the hunger, fatigue, and any spiritual battles that arise, trusting that God is with you every step of the way. As you journey deeper into your fast, remember that perseverance is not just about willpower; it's about relying on God's strength to sustain you.

This chapter will guide you in understanding the importance of perseverance in fasting, how to overcome the challenges you may face, and how to draw strength from God to keep going.

> ## OVERVIEW OF DAY 8:
> ## THE POWER OF PERSEVERANCE

The theme for Day 8 is perseverance—continuing steadfastly despite the challenges that arise. Fasting is a marathon, not a sprint, and like any long journey, it requires endurance. The second week of fasting often brings with it new challenges: the initial novelty has worn off, the physical demands are more noticeable, and spiritual resistance can intensify.

Perseverance is what keeps you moving forward when the journey gets tough. It's the quality that enables you to stay committed to your fast, even when you feel like giving up. As you continue your fast, remember that every challenge you face is an opportunity to grow stronger in your faith and to deepen your reliance on God.

Today is about recognizing the challenges you're facing, acknowledging the difficulty, and choosing to press on with God's help. Perseverance is not about ignoring the struggle; it's about facing it head-on with the assurance that God is your strength and refuge.

> ## SCRIPTURE OF THE DAY: JAMES 1:2-4

Consider it pure joy, my brothers and sisters, whenever you face trials of many kinds, because you know that the testing of your faith produces perseverance. Let perseverance finish its work so that you may be mature and complete, not lacking anything. —James 1:2-4

Today's scripture from the book of James offers a powerful perspective on challenges and perseverance. James encourages us to view trials as opportunities for growth, knowing that they produce perseverance. This perseverance, in turn, leads to spiritual maturity and completeness.

As you meditate on this verse, consider how your fasting journey is testing and strengthening your faith. What challenges are you facing, and how are they helping you to grow? How is God using these challenges to produce perseverance in you?

Perseverance is not just about enduring hardship; it's about allowing the trials you face to shape you into the person God has called you to be. As you continue your fast today, embrace the challenges as opportunities for growth, trusting that God is using them to mature and complete your faith.

> **KEY THOUGHT:**
> **PERSEVERANCE LEADS TO MATURITY.**

Today's key thought is that perseverance leads to maturity. Fasting is a spiritual discipline that tests your faith, and through that testing, produces perseverance. This perseverance is not an end in itself; it's a means to spiritual maturity, making you more complete in your walk with God.

The challenges you face during fasting are not just obstacles to overcome; they are opportunities for growth. Each moment of difficulty is a chance to deepen your trust in God, refine your character, and develop the perseverance that leads to spiritual maturity.

As you reflect on your fasting journey so far, think about the areas where you've been tested. How has God used these challenges to grow your faith? How is He maturing you through the process of perseverance? Embrace the growth that comes from perseverance, knowing that it is making you more complete in Christ.

PRAYER PROMPT:
A PRAYER FOR STRENGTH TO PERSEVERE

Today's prayer focus is on asking God for the strength to persevere through the challenges you're facing. This is an opportunity to surrender your struggles to God and to ask for His help in maintaining your commitment to your fast.

PRAYER PROMPT:

"Lord, I come to You today acknowledging the challenges I'm facing in this fast. I confess that there are moments when I feel weak, tired, and tempted to give up. But I know that You are my strength, and I ask for Your help to persevere. Help me to see these challenges as opportunities for growth, to trust that You are using them to mature my faith. Lord, give me the endurance I need to keep going, to stay committed to this fast, and to continue seeking You with all my heart. I know that You are with me, and I trust that You will carry me through every trial I face. Thank You for the work You are doing in me, even when it's hard. I surrender my struggles to You, and I ask for Your strength to persevere. In Jesus's name, I pray. Amen."

SCIENTIFIC INSIGHT:
PEAK AUTOPHAGY AND EMOTIONAL STABILITY

KEYWORD DEFINITION: PERSEVERANCE

Perseverance is the mental strength to keep going, even when things get tough. It's the ability to stay focused on your goal, pushing through obstacles, discomfort, or setbacks without giving up. In fasting, perseverance helps you overcome initial challenges, like hunger or cravings, allowing you to stick with the practice and experience the deeper benefits. Research shows that perseverance is closely tied to resilience, motivation, and even long-term success, as it builds mental endurance and fosters personal growth.[16]

Today, autophagy is at its peak. Your body is getting rid of all the damaged cells and toxins, promoting serious cellular regeneration. Hormonal levels are stabilizing, leading to greater emotional balance and peace. Make sure you are practicing perseverance.

Perseverance is not just a spiritual concept; it's also a physical and psychological process that involves the brain's ability to maintain focus and motivation despite challenges. Neuroscience has shown that perseverance is linked to the brain's reward system and the regulation of stress responses, both of which are critical during fasting.

The Role of the Brain's Reward System

The brain's reward system, particularly the release of dopamine, plays a significant role in perseverance. Dopamine is a neurotransmitter that motivates behavior by providing a sense of pleasure or satisfaction when you achieve a goal or overcome a challenge. This dopamine release is crucial for maintaining motivation, especially during difficult tasks like fasting.[17]

The anticipation of a reward, such as the spiritual and physical benefits of completing a fast, can increase dopamine levels, thereby enhancing motivation and perseverance. This process helps you to stay committed to your fast, even when the physical and mental challenges intensify.

During fasting, the body's energy levels may fluctuate, and you may experience periods of low motivation or fatigue. However, understanding that your brain's reward system is at work can encourage you to press on, knowing that the perseverance you develop will lead to greater spiritual and emotional rewards.

---

16 Liang Wang, "The Role of Students' Self-Regulated Learning, Grit, and Resilience in Second Language Learning," *Frontiers in Psychology* 12 (2021): 800488, https://doi.org/10.3389/psyg.2021.800488.
17 Jochen Michely et al., "The role of dopamine in dynamic effort-reward integration," *Neuropsychopharmacology* 45, no. 9 (2020): 1448-53, https://doi.org/ 10.1038/s41386-020-0669-0.

Fasting and Mental Resilience

Fasting itself can also enhance mental resilience, as the discipline required to fast trains the brain to tolerate discomfort and delay gratification. This increased resilience can carry over into other areas of your life, helping you to face challenges with greater confidence and perseverance.

As you continue your fast, remember that perseverance is not just a matter of willpower; it's a process that involves both your brain and your spirit. By understanding the physiological aspects of perseverance, you can better navigate the challenges of fasting and stay committed to your spiritual goals.

> **DAY 8 TIP:**
> **HYDRATION FOR DEEP DETOX AND BALANCE**

By Day 8 of your twenty-one-day fast, your body is in a deeper state of detoxification and repair, and water is your best ally in this phase. Drinking enough water today helps flush out toxins that are released as your body burns through stored fats and cleanses itself at a cellular level. Hydration also supports balanced energy levels and can help reduce any physical or mental fatigue you may be experiencing. Aim to sip water consistently throughout the day and consider herbal teas for variety. Staying hydrated will keep you feeling balanced and help your body continue its deep healing process!

> **JOURNALING: REFLECTING ON PERSEVERANCE**

Journaling today provides an opportunity to reflect on the importance of perseverance in your fasting journey. Use this time to document your thoughts, prayers, and any insights you receive about how perseverance is shaping your spiritual and physical well-being.

JOURNALING PROMPTS:

1) What challenges are you facing during this fast? Reflect on the specific difficulties you've encountered so far, whether physical, mental, or spiritual. How are these challenges testing your perseverance?

_____

_____

_____

_____

_____

_____

_____

2) How is God helping you to persevere? Consider the ways in which God has provided strength, encouragement, or insight to help you continue your fast. How is He using these challenges to grow your faith?

_____

_____

_____

_____

_____

_____

_____

3) How does the scientific understanding of perseverance enhance your ability to endure? Think about how the brain's reward system and stress responses influence your perseverance. How can you use this knowledge to stay motivated and resilient during your fast?

4) What prayers of perseverance are on your heart today? Write out a personal prayer asking God to continue strengthening your perseverance. Express your desire to stay committed to your fast and to grow in maturity through the challenges you face.

_____

_____

_____

Journaling helps you to capture the spiritual and physical benefits of perseverance during your fast. It's a way to document your journey, reflect on the growth you're experiencing, and deepen your reliance on God.

ENCOURAGEMENT FOR THE JOURNEY AHEAD

As you conclude Day 8, pause for a moment. Take in what you've already accomplished. Fasting is no easy task, and the fact that you've reached this point is a true testament to your commitment, strength, and faith. You're not just abstaining from food; you're choosing to press into God's presence, grow, and surrender more fully to His will.

Remember, perseverance is a process—a journey that leads to maturity. The challenges you face along the way are not obstacles but opportunities for growth. Each hunger pang, each moment of doubt, is a chance to strengthen your resolve, lean deeper into the grace of God, and cultivate the fruits of the Spirit.

And here's an important truth: perseverance is not about perfection. It's about staying the course, even when the road is difficult. It's about showing up each day, trusting that God's strength is sufficient, even when yours feels depleted. He is using this time to refine you, shape your character, deepen your faith, and draw you ever closer to Him.

Every step of this journey brings you closer to God and more in tune with His heart. As you persevere through the hard moments, remember—you are not alone. God is walking this path with you, providing the strength, wisdom, and encouragement you need. So, take heart and keep going. With each passing day, you are drawing nearer to breakthrough and greater intimacy with your Creator.

You've made it this far, and you're stronger than you know. Let's continue this journey together, trusting that God's grace will carry us all the way through.

> LOOKING AHEAD: **PREPARING FOR DAY 9**

Tomorrow, as you move into Day 9, the focus will be on spiritual discernment. Fasting often heightens your spiritual sensitivity, making it an ideal time to seek God's guidance and direction. On Day 9, you'll explore how to discern God's voice more clearly and how to apply His wisdom to your life.

As you prepare for tomorrow, give thanks to God for continuing to guide you and give you the strength to persevere in this transformative journey.

CHAPTER 10

DAY 9

CULTIVATING SPIRITUAL DISCERNMENT

THE IMPORTANCE OF DISCERNMENT

Welcome to Day 9 of your fasting journey. As you've progressed through your fast, you've likely noticed an increase in your spiritual awareness and sensitivity. Fasting has a unique way of clearing the spiritual "fog" that often clouds our ability to hear from God and perceive His guidance. Today's focus is on cultivating spiritual discernment, a crucial aspect of your walk with God that enables you to navigate life's challenges with wisdom and clarity.

Discernment is the ability to understand and distinguish between different spiritual influences, recognize God's voice, and make decisions that align with His will. It's a spiritual gift that becomes sharper with practice, especially during times of fasting and prayer. As you continue your fast, you're invited to lean into this gift, seek God's guidance more intentionally, and trust that He will lead you in the right direction.

This chapter will guide you in understanding the role of spiritual discernment in fasting, how to cultivate it, and how to apply it to your daily life.

> **OVERVIEW OF DAY 9:
> SHARPENING YOUR SPIRITUAL SENSES**

The theme for Day 9 is cultivating spiritual discernment—sharpening your ability to hear God's voice and understand His will. Fasting is a powerful tool for enhancing spiritual discernment because it removes distractions, quiets the noise of the world, and creates space for God to speak.

Spiritual discernment is not just about making decisions; it's about developing a deep, ongoing relationship with God where you can recognize His guidance in every aspect of your life. As you fast, your spiritual senses become more attuned to His presence, making it easier to discern His direction.

Today is about embracing this heightened sensitivity, seeking God's wisdom, and learning to trust the discernment He gives you. Whether you're facing a specific decision or simply seeking to grow in your understanding of God's will, this is an opportunity to draw closer to Him and listen more carefully to His voice.

> **SCRIPTURE OF THE DAY: PROVERBS 3:5-6**

"Trust in the LORD with all your heart and lean not on your own understanding; in all your ways submit to him, and he will make your paths straight."—Proverbs 3:5-6 Today's scripture from Proverbs emphasizes the importance of trusting in God's wisdom rather than relying on your own understanding. Spiritual discernment begins with a heart that is fully surrendered to God, trusting that He knows the best path for your life.

As you meditate on this verse, consider the areas of your life where you need God's guidance. Are there decisions you're facing that require His wisdom? How can you submit your ways to Him and trust that He will direct your paths?

Discernment is about leaning on God rather than your own understanding. It's about acknowledging that His ways are higher than your ways and that His wisdom surpasses human knowledge. Today, let this verse guide you into a deeper trust in God's direction and a greater openness to His leading.

> **KEY THOUGHT:**
> **DISCERNMENT REQUIRES SURRENDER.**

Today's key thought is that true spiritual discernment requires surrender. To cultivate discernment, you must be willing to let go of your own desires, plans, and preconceived notions, and fully trust in God's wisdom. This surrender is not a one-time act but a daily practice of submitting your thoughts, decisions, and life to God.

Fasting is a practice that naturally leads to this kind of surrender. As you abstain from food and other comforts, you're reminded of your dependence on God and your need for His guidance. This surrender creates the perfect environment for discernment to flourish, as it clears away the clutter and allows you to focus more clearly on God's voice.

As you move through today, reflect on the areas where you need to surrender more fully to God's guidance. How can you trust Him more deeply, and how can you cultivate the kind of spiritual discernment that comes from a heart fully yielded to Him?

> ### PRAYER PROMPT: A PRAYER FOR DISCERNMENT

Today's prayer focus is on asking God for the gift of discernment. This is an opportunity to seek His wisdom, ask for clarity in the decisions you face, and trust that He will lead you in the right direction.

PRAYER PROMPT:

"Lord, I come to You today, acknowledging my need for Your wisdom and guidance. I confess that I often rely on my own understanding, but I want to trust in You with all my heart. Help me to surrender my thoughts, my plans, and my decisions to You. Lord, I ask for the gift of discernment, that I may recognize Your voice and follow Your leading in every area of my life. Give me clarity in the choices I face and the wisdom to discern what is right and pleasing to You. Thank You for being a faithful guide, for always leading me on the path that is best. I trust that You will make my paths straight as I submit my ways to You. In Jesus's name, I pray. Amen."

> ### SCIENTIFIC INSIGHT: DEEP HEALING AND CONTINUED CELLULAR REPAIR

KEYWORD DEFINITION: DECISION-MAKING

Decision-making is the process your brain uses to evaluate options and choose the best course of action. It involves various parts of the brain, especially the prefrontal cortex, which is responsible for weighing pros and cons, managing impulses, and planning ahead. When fasting, you might find that your decision-making feels sharper or, at times, more challenging, depending on your body's energy levels. This is because the availability of glucose, a primary energy source for the brain, affects cognitive functions, including making decisions.[18]

Your body is in deep repair mode, with continued autophagy reducing inflammation and healing tissues. Mentally, you're likely feeling sharp and focused. Emotionally, there's a calmness that comes from the steadying of hormones.

THE NEUROSCIENCE OF DECISION-MAKING AND SPIRITUAL DISCERNMENT

The process of decision-making, particularly in the context of spiritual discernment, is not just a spiritual exercise but also involves complex neurological functions. Neuroscience has provided insights into how the brain processes information and makes decisions, and how practices like prayer and meditation can enhance these abilities.

The Role of the Prefrontal Cortex in Decision-Making

The prefrontal cortex is the part of the brain responsible for higher-order thinking, including decision-making, problem-solving, and impulse control. This area of the brain is crucial for spiritual discernment, as it allows you to weigh options, consider consequences, and make choices that align with your values and beliefs.

Research published in *the Zygon®* indicates that activities such as prayer can enhance the overall functioning of our mental health. There is a greater anterior activation values and increased blood flow to frontal sites during prayer and meditation.[19] During fasting, the reduced intake of food can also impact glucose levels, which the brain relies on for energy. However, the body's adaptation to fasting, including the production of ketones, provides an alternative and more stable energy source for the brain, particularly for the prefrontal

---
18 Joshua I. Gold and Michael N. Shadlen, "The Neural Basis of Decision Making," *Annual Review Neuroscience* 30, no. 1 (2007): 535-74, https://doi.org/ 10.1146/annurev.neuro.29.051605.113038.
19 Patrick McNamara, "The Motivational Origins of Religious Practices," *Zygon®* 37, no. 1 (2002): 143-60, https://doi.org/10.1111/1467-9744.00418.

cortex. This shift can lead to improved mental clarity and decision-making during prolonged fasting periods.

> ### DAY 9 TIP: **WATER FOR SUSTAINED ENERGY AND MENTAL CLARITY**

On Day 9 of your twenty-one-day fast, hydration remains essential for keeping your energy stable and your mind clear. As your body continues deep detox and adapts to relying on stored energy, water helps flush out accumulated waste and supports smooth digestion. Drinking water throughout the day can reduce any feelings of sluggishness, keep you mentally sharp, and support your body's natural healing processes. Try to keep water within easy reach and sip regularly—hydration at this stage is not only vital for comfort but also for maximizing the benefits of your fast.

> ### JOURNALING: **REFLECTING ON DISCERNMENT**

Journaling today provides an opportunity to reflect on the role of discernment in your fasting journey. Use this time to document your thoughts, prayers, and any insights you receive about how discernment is shaping your spiritual and decision-making processes.

JOURNALING PROMPTS:

1) What decisions are you facing that require discernment? Reflect on any specific choices or situations where you need God's guidance. How are you seeking His wisdom in these areas?

_____

_____

2) How is fasting helping you to cultivate spiritual discernment? Consider how the clarity and focus you're experiencing during this fast are impacting your ability to hear God's voice. How is this discernment influencing your decisions?

3) How does the scientific understanding of decision-making enhance your approach to spiritual discernment? Think about how the brain's role in decision-making aligns with the spiritual practice of discernment. How can you use this knowledge to improve your discernment during your fast?

4) What prayers of discernment are on your heart today? Write out a personal prayer asking God to continue sharpening your spiritual discernment. Express your desire to follow His guidance and to make decisions that align with His will.

Journaling helps you to capture the spiritual and cognitive benefits of discernment during your fast. It's a way to document your journey, reflect on the insights you're gaining, and deepen your connection with God's wisdom.

ENCOURAGEMENT FOR THE JOURNEY AHEAD

As you conclude Day 9, take a moment to acknowledge the growth in spiritual discernment you've experienced during this fast. Fasting is not just about abstaining from food; it's about creating space for God to speak and for you to hear His voice more clearly. Each day of your fast brings you closer to God and sharpens your ability to discern His will.

Remember that discernment is both a gift and a skill—one that is cultivated through prayer, meditation, and a deep reliance on God. As you continue your fast, trust that God is guiding you, that He is sharpening your spiritual senses, and that He is leading you on the path that is best for you.

Each day of your fasting journey brings you closer to God and deeper into His presence. As you cultivate discernment, know that you are not alone; God is with you, providing the wisdom and guidance you need to navigate your path.

LOOKING AHEAD: **PREPARING FOR DAY 10**

Tomorrow, as you move into Day 10, the focus will be on spiritual warfare. Fasting often brings heightened spiritual awareness, but it can also lead to increased spiritual opposition. On Day 10, you'll explore how to recognize and respond to spiritual warfare, using the strength and discernment you've developed to stand firm in your faith.

As you prepare for tomorrow, ask God to continue guiding you and to give you the strength and discernment to face any challenges that may come your way.

CHAPTER 11

DAY 10

STANDING FIRM IN SPIRITUAL WARFARE

UNDERSTANDING SPIRITUAL WARFARE

Welcome to Day 10 of your fasting journey. As you continue to deepen your spiritual walk through fasting and prayer, it's important to recognize that this journey often comes with its own set of challenges—particularly in the form of spiritual warfare. Spiritual warfare refers to the battles we face against the forces of darkness that seek to oppose God's work in our lives. Today's focus is on standing firm in spiritual warfare, using the spiritual strength and discernment you've cultivated to resist the enemy's attacks and remain steadfast in your faith.

Fasting often heightens spiritual awareness, making you more attuned to both the presence of God and the tactics of the enemy. This increased sensitivity can sometimes lead to a greater sense of opposition, as the enemy seeks to disrupt your progress and discourage you from continuing your fast. However, the Bible assures us that we are equipped with the armor of God to stand firm against these attacks and to emerge victorious.

This chapter will guide you in understanding the nature of spiritual warfare, how to recognize the enemy's tactics, and how to use the spiritual armor God has provided to stand strong in the face of opposition.

OVERVIEW OF DAY 10: **EQUIPPED FOR BATTLE**

The theme for Day 10 is standing firm in spiritual warfare. Fasting is not just a physical discipline; it's a spiritual one that can provoke spiritual resistance. The enemy often targets believers who are actively pursuing God, especially during times of fasting and prayer, because these practices strengthen your faith and draw you closer to God.

Understanding spiritual warfare is crucial for maintaining your spiritual ground. The Bible describes the Christian life as a battle, not against flesh and blood, but against spiritual forces of evil (Ephesians 6:12). This battle requires spiritual weapons—prayer, the Word of God, and the armor of God—to protect you and help you stand firm.

Today is about recognizing the spiritual opposition you may face, understanding the tactics of the enemy, and confidently using the spiritual tools God has given you to resist and overcome. It's a day to reaffirm your commitment to your fast and to trust that God is fighting for you.

SCRIPTURE OF THE DAY: **EPHESIANS 6:10-11**

"Finally, be strong in the Lord and in his mighty power. Put on the full armor of God, so that you can take your stand against the devil's schemes."—Ephesians 6:10-11

Today's scripture from Ephesians is a powerful reminder of the strength and protection we have in God. Paul urges believers to be strong in the Lord and to put on the full armor of God so that they can stand firm against the enemy's schemes. This armor includes truth, righteousness, the gospel of peace, faith, salvation, the Word of God, and prayer.

As you meditate on this verse, consider how you are equipping yourself with the armor of God during this fast. Are there areas where you feel vulnerable to attack? How can you use the spiritual weapons God has given you to stand firm?

Spiritual warfare is a reality of the Christian life, but God has not left us defenseless. He has provided everything we need to stand firm and resist the enemy's attacks. Today, let this verse encourage you to take up the armor of God and rely on His mighty power to protect and strengthen you.

> **KEY THOUGHT: SPIRITUAL WARFARE REQUIRES SPIRITUAL ARMOR.**

Today's key thought is that spiritual warfare requires spiritual armor. Just as a soldier would never go into battle without the proper gear, a believer should never face spiritual warfare without being fully equipped with the armor of God. This armor is not physical but spiritual, designed to protect your heart, mind, and spirit from the enemy's attacks.

The armor of God is detailed in Ephesians 6:13-18, and it includes the belt of truth, the breastplate of righteousness, the gospel of peace, the shield of faith, the helmet of salvation, the sword of the Spirit, and prayer. Each piece of armor serves a specific purpose in defending against spiritual attacks and in standing firm in the face of opposition.

As you move through today, reflect on how you can actively put on the armor of God. How can you strengthen your faith, immerse yourself in God's Word, and stand firm in truth and righteousness? Remember that spiritual warfare is not fought with physical strength but with the spiritual power that comes from God.

> **PRAYER PROMPT: A PRAYER FOR SPIRITUAL PROTECTION**

Today's prayer focus is on asking God for spiritual protection and strength to stand firm in the face of spiritual warfare. This is an opportunity to pray through each piece of the armor of God and to ask for His protection over your mind, heart, and spirit.

PRAYER PROMPT:

"Father, I come to You today recognizing the reality of spiritual warfare and my need for Your protection. I thank You for the armor You have provided and for the promise that You are with me in every battle. Lord, I put on the belt of truth, standing firm in Your Word. I wear the breastplate of righteousness, trusting in the righteousness of Christ. I fit my feet with the gospel of peace, ready to stand firm in the good news of Your salvation. I take up the shield of faith, extinguishing all the fiery arrows of the enemy. I put on the helmet of salvation, guarding my mind with the assurance of my salvation. I wield the sword of the Spirit, Your Word, which is living and active. And I pray in the Spirit on all occasions, asking for Your strength and guidance. Lord, protect me from the enemy's schemes and help me to stand firm in Your mighty power. Thank You for being my shield and my refuge. In Jesus's name, I pray. Amen."

> SCIENTIFIC INSIGHT: **ENHANCED IMMUNE FUNCTION AND EMOTIONAL BALANCE**

KEYWORD DEFINITION: AMYGDALA

The amygdala is a small, almond-shaped cluster of neurons in your brain that plays a key role in processing emotions, especially fear and stress. Think of it as your emotional response center—when you encounter something threatening or stressful, the amygdala kicks into gear, signaling your body to react, often with a "fight-or-flight" response. During fasting, the amygdala's activity can sometimes increase, especially if you're facing hunger-related stress, but many people also find that fasting over time helps them manage stress better and feel calmer.[20]

Your immune system is getting a significant boost right now, thanks to ongoing autophagy. This process reduces inflammation and enhances your body's ability to fight off disease. Emotionally, you should be feeling balanced and more at peace.

Tip: Keep drinking water to support your immune system and help your body continue its detoxification. Just as your immune system is being strengthened, let your spiritual defenses be fortified as you continue to grow in faith and resilience.

THE PSYCHOLOGICAL IMPACT OF SPIRITUAL WARFARE AND RESILIENCE

Spiritual warfare, while primarily a spiritual experience, also has significant psychological effects. The challenges and opposition faced during spiritual warfare can lead to increased stress, anxiety, and mental fatigue. Understanding the psychological impact of spiritual warfare and how resilience

---

20 Karine Sergerie, "The role of the amygdala in emotional processing: A quantitative meta-analysis of functional neuroimaging studies," *Neuroscience & Biobehavioral Reviews* 32, no. 4 (2008): 811-30, https://doi.org/10.1016/j.neubiorev.2007.12.002.

can be built through spiritual practices is essential for maintaining mental and emotional well-being.

The Role of the Amygdala in Fear and Stress

The amygdala is a region of the brain that plays a key role in processing emotions, particularly fear and stress. During times of spiritual warfare, when individuals may feel attacked or threatened, the amygdala can become highly active, leading to heightened feelings of fear, anxiety, and vigilance.

The Impact of Resilience on Spiritual Warfare

Resilience is the ability to bounce back from adversity and maintain psychological and emotional stability during challenging times. In the context of spiritual warfare, resilience is essential for standing firm against the enemy's attacks and for maintaining faith and focus.

Resilience is not just about enduring; it's about thriving in the midst of adversity. By strengthening your resilience through spiritual practices, you can better navigate the psychological and spiritual challenges of spiritual warfare, standing firm in your faith and emerging stronger on the other side.

Fasting and the Strengthening of Resilience

Fasting itself is a discipline that builds resilience, both physically and spiritually. The act of denying oneself food and other comforts requires mental strength and perseverance, which translate into greater resilience in the face of spiritual challenges. As you continue your fast, you are not only building spiritual strength but also enhancing your mental and emotional resilience.

As you stand firm in spiritual warfare, remember that the resilience you are building through fasting and prayer is equipping you to face any challenge with confidence and strength.

DAY 10 TIP:
HYDRATION FOR ENDURANCE AND CLEANSING

On Day 10 of your twenty-one-day fast, staying hydrated is crucial as your body continues its deep cleanse and adapts to extended fasting. Drinking water helps flush out toxins that are being released from fat stores, supporting your liver and kidneys in their vital detox work. Proper hydration also sustains your energy levels and prevents dehydration-related fatigue or headaches, which can be more noticeable as the fast progresses. Keep water nearby and sip steadily throughout the day—this simple habit is key to maintaining endurance, supporting mental clarity, and maximizing the benefits of your fast!

JOURNALING:
REFLECTING ON SPIRITUAL WARFARE

Journaling today provides an opportunity to reflect on the reality of spiritual warfare in your fasting journey. Use this time to document your thoughts, prayers, and any insights you receive about how spiritual warfare is impacting your spiritual and psychological well-being.

JOURNALING PROMPTS:

1) What signs of spiritual warfare have you experienced during this fast? Reflect on any challenges, doubts, or opposition you've faced that may be linked to spiritual warfare. How are you responding to these challenges?

_____

_____

_____

2) How is God equipping you to stand firm in spiritual warfare? Consider the ways in which God is strengthening you through prayer, scripture, and the armor of God. How are these spiritual tools helping you to resist the enemy's attacks?

3) How does the scientific understanding of stress and resilience enhance your approach to spiritual warfare? Think about how the brain's response to stress and the role of resilience align with the spiritual practice of standing firm in warfare. How can you use this knowledge to maintain mental and emotional stability during your fast?

4) What prayers of protection and resilience are on your heart today? Write out a personal prayer asking God to protect you from the enemy's schemes and to strengthen your resilience in the face of spiritual warfare. Express your trust in His power to guard and guide you.

Journaling helps you to capture the spiritual and psychological dynamics of spiritual warfare during your fast. It's a way to document your journey, reflect on the resilience you're building, and deepen your reliance on God's protection and strength.

ENCOURAGEMENT FOR THE JOURNEY AHEAD

As you conclude Day 10, take a moment to recognize the strength and resilience you are developing through this fast. Spiritual warfare is a reality for every believer, but with the armor of God and the power of His Spirit, you are equipped to stand firm and overcome. Remember that you are not fighting this battle alone—God is with you, and He is your shield and defender.

As you continue your fast, lean on the truth that God is your refuge and strength, an ever-present help in trouble. Trust that He will protect you from the enemy's attacks and that He will give you the strength to persevere and to emerge victorious.

Each day of your fasting journey is a step closer to victory in Christ. As you stand firm in spiritual warfare, know that you are growing stronger in your faith and deeper in your relationship with God.

LOOKING AHEAD: PREPARING FOR DAY 11

Tomorrow, as you move into Day 11, the focus will shift to cultivating a spirit of gratitude. Fasting often heightens your awareness of God's blessings and grace, making it an ideal time to develop a deeper sense of thankfulness. On Day 11, you'll explore how gratitude can transform your fasting experience and draw you closer to God.

As you prepare for tomorrow, ask God to open your heart to His goodness and to help you cultivate a spirit of gratitude, even in the midst of challenges.

CHAPTER 12

DAY 11

CULTIVATING A SPIRIT OF GRATITUDE

THE POWER OF GRATITUDE

Welcome to Day 11 of your fasting journey. As you enter this new phase of your fast, it's time to focus on cultivating a spirit of gratitude. Fasting often brings challenges, but it also provides a unique opportunity to recognize and appreciate the many blessings in your life. Gratitude is a powerful spiritual practice that can transform your fasting experience, helping you to see God's hand at work in even the smallest details.

Gratitude shifts your perspective from what you lack to what you have, from the challenges you face to the blessings you receive. It opens your heart to God's goodness and deepens your relationship with Him. Today, you're invited to intentionally cultivate gratitude, reflect on the many ways God has blessed you, and express your thanks to Him.

This chapter will guide you in understanding the importance of gratitude during fasting, how to cultivate it, and how it can enhance your spiritual growth and overall well-being.

OVERVIEW OF DAY 11: THE TRANSFORMATIVE POWER OF GRATITUDE

The theme for Day 11 is cultivating a spirit of gratitude—a mindset that recognizes and celebrates the blessings in your life, even in the midst of challenges. Fasting can sometimes bring discomfort, but it also heightens your awareness of God's presence and provision. Gratitude is the key to unlocking the joy and peace that come from acknowledging God's goodness.

Gratitude is more than just saying "thank you;" it's a deep-seated attitude that shapes the way you see the world and interact with others. It's a recognition that everything you have—your health, your relationships, your opportunities—comes from God's hand. As you cultivate gratitude, you'll find that it transforms your perspective, bringing you closer to God and filling your heart with joy.

Today is about embracing gratitude as a way of life, using it to fuel your fast and to draw nearer to God. Whether you're reflecting on the past, considering the present, or looking forward to the future, let gratitude guide your thoughts and actions.

SCRIPTURE OF THE DAY: 1 THESSALONIANS 5:16-18

"Rejoice always, pray continually, give thanks in all circumstances; for this is God's will for you in Christ Jesus."—1 Thessalonians 5:16-18

Today's scripture from 1 Thessalonians emphasizes the importance of rejoicing, praying, and giving thanks in all circumstances. This verse reminds us that gratitude is not dependent on our circumstances but is a choice we make in response to God's faithfulness and love.

As you meditate on this verse, consider how you can give thanks in your current situation. What blessings can you celebrate today? How can you express your gratitude to God for His goodness, even in the midst of challenges?

Gratitude is a powerful tool for maintaining a positive and hopeful attitude, regardless of your circumstances. Today, let this verse inspire you to cultivate a spirit of gratitude, rejoice in God's presence, and give thanks in all things.

> **KEY THOUGHT:**
> **GRATITUDE TRANSFORMS PERSPECTIVE.**

Today's key thought is that gratitude transforms your perspective. When you focus on what you're thankful for, you begin to see your life through the lens of God's grace and provision. Gratitude shifts your focus from what you lack to what you have, from the struggles you face to the blessings you receive.

This shift in perspective is essential during fasting, as it helps you to maintain a positive and hopeful attitude. Instead of dwelling on the discomforts of fasting, gratitude encourages you to focus on the spiritual growth and blessings that come from this discipline.

As you move through today, reflect on the ways that gratitude is transforming your perspective. How is it helping you to see God's hand at work in your life? How is it bringing you closer to Him? Embrace the power of gratitude, knowing that it has the ability to change the way you see the world and to deepen your relationship with God.

> **PRAYER PROMPT: A PRAYER OF THANKSGIVING**

Today's prayer focus is on expressing your gratitude to God. This is an opportunity to thank Him for His many blessings, recognize His goodness, and offer praise for all that He has done in your life.

PRAYER PROMPT:

"Father, I come to You today with a heart full of gratitude. I thank You for Your many blessings, for the ways You have provided for me, guided me, and protected me. Lord, I thank You for the gift of this fast, for the spiritual growth and the closeness to You that it has brought. Help me to see Your hand at work in every area of my life, to recognize the blessings that I often take for granted, and to give thanks in all circumstances. I praise You for Your faithfulness, for Your love, and for the peace that comes from knowing You. Lord, fill my heart with gratitude, and let it overflow in praise and thanksgiving. In Jesus's name, I pray. Amen."

> **SCIENTIFIC INSIGHT: MAXIMIZING CELLULAR REPAIR AND GROWTH HORMONE SURGE**

KEYWORD DEFINITION: GROWTH HORMONE

Growth hormone (GH) is a powerful protein hormone produced by the pituitary gland that plays a key role in growth, cell repair, and metabolism. Think of it as your body's renewal and regeneration hormone—it promotes the growth of tissues, aids in muscle repair, and helps break down fat for energy. During fasting, GH levels naturally increase, as the body shifts into repair mode. This boost in growth hormone supports fat burning, muscle preservation, and cellular repair, making it essential for maintaining overall health and vitality.[21]

Autophagy and cellular repair are at their peak, and your body is producing a surge of growth hormones that help with muscle preservation and fat loss. Your body's resilience is increasing, and you're becoming more adapted to the fasting state.

The Neuroscience of Gratitude

Gratitude is not only a spiritual practice but also a powerful tool for enhancing mental and emotional well-being. Neuroscientific research has shown that cultivating gratitude can lead to significant positive changes in the brain, impacting your mood, relationships, and overall quality of life.

The Role of the Brain's Reward System in Gratitude

Gratitude activates the brain's reward system, particularly the release of dopamine and serotonin, two neurotransmitters associated with feelings of pleasure, happiness, and well-being. When you practice gratitude, your brain releases these chemicals, creating a sense of satisfaction and contentment.[22]

By focusing on what you're thankful for, you can literally rewire your brain to become more positive, resilient, and optimistic. This is particularly beneficial during fasting, as it helps you to maintain a positive attitude despite the physical and mental challenges you may face.

Fasting, Gratitude, and Spiritual Growth

Fasting provides a unique opportunity to cultivate gratitude, as it strips away distractions and helps you to focus on what truly matters. When you fast, you become more aware of God's provision, the blessings in your life, and the many ways He cares for you. This heightened awareness naturally leads to a deeper sense of gratitude.

---

21 "Growth hormone," *BetterHealth Channel*, https://www.betterhealth.vic.gov.au/health/conditionsandtreatments/growth-hormone.
22 Madhuleena Roy Chowdhury, "The Neuroscience of Gratitude and Effects on the Brain," *PositivePsychology.com*, 9 Apr. 2019, https://positivepsychology.com/neuroscience-of-gratitude/.

As you continue your fast, remember that gratitude is a powerful tool for deepening your spiritual growth and enhancing your overall well-being. By focusing on what you're thankful for, you can transform your fasting experience and draw closer to God.

> ### DAY 11 TIP: **HYDRATION FOR DEEP DETOX AND MENTAL FOCUS**

By Day 11 of your twenty-one-day fast, your body is likely deep into detox mode, breaking down stored fats and releasing waste products. Drinking water is essential to flush out these toxins, supporting your liver and kidneys in their cleansing work. Proper hydration also helps maintain mental focus and reduces any lingering fatigue, making it easier to stay clear-headed and engaged. Aim to drink water steadily throughout the day, and if you'd like a change, try adding a slice of lemon or a splash of apple cider vinegar for extra detox support. Each sip is aiding your body in this powerful cleansing journey!

> ### JOURNALING: **REFLECTING ON GRATITUDE**

Journaling today provides an opportunity to reflect on the role of gratitude in your fasting journey. Use this time to document your thoughts, prayers, and any insights you receive about how gratitude is shaping your spiritual and emotional well-being.

JOURNALING PROMPTS:

1) What are you thankful for today? Reflect on the specific blessings, both big and small, that you've experienced during your fast. How has God provided for you, guided you, or shown His love?

_____

_____

_____

_____

_____

_____

_____

2) How is gratitude transforming your perspective? Consider how focusing on gratitude is changing the way you see your life, your challenges, and your relationship with God. How is it helping you to maintain a positive and hopeful attitude during your fast?

_____

_____

_____

_____

_____

_____

_____

3) How does the scientific understanding of gratitude enhance your spiritual practice? Think about how the brain's response to gratitude aligns with the spiritual practice of giving thanks. How can you use this knowledge to deepen your gratitude during your fast?

_____
_____
_____
_____
_____
_____
_____

4) What prayers of thanksgiving are on your heart today? Write out a personal prayer expressing your gratitude to God. Thank Him for His blessings, His guidance, and His presence in your life.

_____
_____
_____
_____
_____
_____
_____

Journaling helps you to capture the spiritual and emotional benefits of gratitude during your fast. It's a way to document your journey, reflect on the blessings you're receiving, and deepen your connection with God through thanksgiving.

ENCOURAGEMENT FOR THE JOURNEY AHEAD

As you conclude Day 11, take a moment to bask in the warmth of gratitude. Cultivating a spirit of thankfulness during your fast not only transforms your perspective but also draws you closer to God, opening your heart to the fullness of His grace and love. Remember that gratitude is a powerful tool for maintaining joy and peace, even in the midst of challenges.

As you continue your fast, let gratitude be the lens through which you view your life and your relationship with God. Trust that He is with you, blessing you, and guiding you every step of the way.

Each day of your fasting journey is an opportunity to grow in gratitude and to experience the transformative power of thankfulness. As you cultivate a spirit of gratitude, know that you are aligning your heart with God's goodness and opening yourself to receive even more of His blessings.

LOOKING AHEAD: **PREPARING FOR DAY 12**

Tomorrow, as you move into Day 12, the focus will shift to the theme of humility. Fasting naturally leads to a posture of humility, reminding us of our dependence on God and our need for His grace. On Day 12, you'll explore how humility deepens your relationship with God and enhances your spiritual growth.

As you prepare for tomorrow, ask God to cultivate in you a heart of humility, help you recognize your need for His grace, and lead you into a deeper relationship with Him. Trust that He is with you, guiding you, and transforming you through this journey.

CHAPTER 13

DAY 12

EMBRACING HUMILITY

THE POWER OF HUMILITY

Welcome to Day 12 of your fasting journey. As you progress through your fast, you may have already experienced a growing awareness of your dependence on God. Fasting naturally brings about a sense of humility, reminding us that we are not self-sufficient and that we rely on God for our strength, provision, and wisdom. Today's focus is on embracing humility, a posture that deepens your relationship with God and enhances your spiritual growth.

Humility is not about thinking less of yourself; it's about thinking of yourself less and recognizing your true position before God. It's an acknowledgment that every good thing comes from Him and that without His grace, we are nothing. Fasting is a powerful tool for cultivating humility because it strips away the layers of self-reliance and pride, bringing you to a place where you can fully surrender to God's will.

This chapter will guide you in understanding the importance of humility during fasting, how to cultivate it, and how it can lead to a deeper, more authentic relationship with God.

OVERVIEW OF DAY 12: THE PATH OF HUMILITY

The theme for Day 12 is embracing humility—a key aspect of spiritual growth that involves recognizing our dependence on God and submitting to His authority. Fasting is a spiritual discipline that naturally leads to humility by highlighting our physical and spiritual needs. When we fast, we are reminded of our human limitations and our need for God's strength and provision.

Humility is essential for a healthy spiritual life because it keeps us grounded in the truth of who we are before God. It allows us to receive His grace, learn from His wisdom, and grow in our faith. As you continue your fast, today is about leaning into this posture of humility, allowing it to shape your heart and guide your actions.

Today is an invitation to set aside pride, acknowledge your need for God, and embrace the humility that fasting brings. As you do so, you'll find that humility opens the door to a deeper, more intimate relationship with God.

SCRIPTURE OF THE DAY: JAMES 4:10

"Humble yourselves before the Lord, and he will lift you up."—James 4:10

Today's scripture from James is a powerful reminder of the promise that comes with humility. When we humble ourselves before the Lord, He promises to lift us up. This verse emphasizes the importance of submitting to God's will and trusting that He will exalt us in His perfect timing.

As you meditate on this verse, consider what it means to humble yourself before God. Are there areas of your life where pride has taken root? How can you surrender these areas to God and trust Him to lift you up?

Humility is not a sign of weakness; it's a pathway to true strength and honor. Today, let this verse guide you into a deeper posture of humility, where you can experience God's grace and be lifted up in His presence.

> KEY THOUGHT: **HUMILITY LEADS TO EXALTATION.**

Today's key thought is that humility leads to exaltation. In God's kingdom, the way up is down—those who humble themselves before God are the ones He lifts up. This paradoxical truth is central to the Christian life and is vividly illustrated through the practice of fasting.

Fasting humbles us by reminding us of our dependence on God. It strips away our illusions of self-sufficiency and brings us face-to-face with our need for His grace and strength. As you embrace humility through fasting, you position yourself to receive God's exaltation—not necessarily in the form of worldly success, but in the form of spiritual growth, deeper intimacy with God, and greater alignment with His will.

As you move through today, reflect on how humility is shaping your relationship with God. How is it helping you to surrender your will to His? How is it leading to a deeper experience of His grace and love? Embrace the humility that fasting brings, trusting that as you lower yourself before God, He will lift you up.

> **PRAYER PROMPT: A PRAYER FOR HUMILITY**

Today's prayer focus is on asking God to cultivate a spirit of humility in your heart. This is an opportunity to surrender your pride, acknowledge your dependence on God, and ask for His grace to walk in humility each day.

PRAYER PROMPT:

"Father, I come to You today, recognizing my need for humility. I confess that there are times when pride takes root in my heart, when I rely on my own strength rather than on You. Lord, I ask that You would humble me, that You would remind me of my dependence on You for every breath, every provision, and every bit of wisdom. Help me to see myself as You see me, not more than I am, but also not less. I surrender my pride to You, and I ask for the grace to walk in humility each day. Thank You for the promise that as I humble myself before You, You will lift me up. I trust in Your timing, in Your plans, and in Your ways. In Jesus's name, I pray. Amen."

> **SCIENTIFIC INSIGHT:**
> **MENTAL AND PHYSICAL HARMONY**

KEYWORD DEFINITION: HUMILITY

Humility is the quality of having a modest view of one's own importance, often accompanied by openness to learning and self-improvement. Scientifically, humility can be thought of as a mental framework that fosters personal growth and resilience by keeping one's ego in check, making it easier to accept feedback, learn from others, and adjust to new information. In fasting, humility can play a subtle but powerful role, helping you stay grounded, focused, and open to the mental and spiritual shifts that can come with this process.[23]

Today, you should feel a harmonious balance between your mind and body. Your brain is functioning optimally on ketones, and your body is comfortably settled into the rhythm of fasting. Everything feels like it's working together smoothly.

THE PSYCHOLOGICAL BENEFITS OF HUMILITY

Humility is not only a spiritual virtue; it also has significant psychological benefits. Research in psychology has shown that humility is associated with greater mental health, better relationships, and a more accurate self-assessment.[24] Embracing humility can lead to a more balanced and fulfilling life, both spiritually and emotionally. Humility allows you to accept your limitations and to seek help when needed, whether from God or from others. This openness to support is crucial for maintaining emotional stability and resilience, especially during challenging times like fasting.

Humility allows you to approach others with a sense of equality and respect, leading to deeper connections and less conflict. This is particularly important during fasting, a time when emotions can run high, and relationships can be tested. By cultivating humility, you can enhance your interactions with others and foster a spirit of unity and peace.

Fasting naturally cultivates humility by bringing you to a place of dependence on God. The physical act of denying yourself food and other comforts serves as a powerful reminder of your limitations and your need for God's strength. As you continue your fast, remember that humility is both a result of fasting and a key to deepening your relationship with God. By embracing

---

23 Rob Nielsen and Jennifer A. Marrone, "Humility: Our Current Understanding of the Construct and its Role in Organizations," *International Journal of Management Reviews* 20 (2018): 805-24, https://doi.org/10.1111/ijmr.12160.
24 Jennifer Cole Wright et al., "The psychological significance of humility," *The Journal of Positive Psychology* 12, no. 1 (2016): 3-12, https://doi.org/10.1080/17439760.2016.1167940.

humility, you open yourself to God's grace, wisdom, and guidance, allowing Him to lift you up in ways that truly matter.

> ### DAY 12 TIP: **HYDRATION FOR CELLULAR HEALTH AND SUSTAINED ENERGY**

On Day 12 of your twenty-one-day fast, drinking water remains a vital component of your journey. As your body is continually working to cleanse and renew at a cellular level, hydration supports this deep cellular repair and helps transport nutrients more effectively. Staying well-hydrated also sustains your energy and focus, reducing feelings of fatigue that can sometimes arise during an extended fast. Keep water within reach today and sip steadily—your cells thrive with each drink, supporting you as you continue to experience the transformative effects of fasting!

> ### JOURNALING: **REFLECTING ON HUMILITY**

Journaling today provides an opportunity to reflect on the role of humility in your fasting journey. Use this time to document your thoughts, prayers, and any insights you receive about how humility is shaping your spiritual and emotional well-being.

JOURNALING PROMPTS:

1) In what areas of your life do you need to cultivate humility? Reflect on any specific areas where pride may have taken root. How can you surrender these areas to God and embrace a posture of humility?

_____

_____

2) How is humility enhancing your relationship with God? Consider how fasting is helping you to recognize your dependence on God and to submit to His will. How is this humility deepening your connection with Him?

3) How does the scientific understanding of humility enhance your spiritual practice? Think about how the psychological benefits of humility align with the spiritual practice of surrendering to God. How can you use this knowledge to cultivate humility during your fast?

4) What prayers of humility are on your heart today? Write out a personal prayer asking God to help you walk in humility each day. Express your desire to rely on His strength and to be lifted up according to His will.

Journaling helps you to capture the spiritual and emotional benefits of humility during your fast. It's a way to document your journey, reflect on the growth you're experiencing, and deepen your connection with God through surrender.

ENCOURAGEMENT FOR THE JOURNEY AHEAD

As you conclude Day 12, take a moment to recognize the strength that comes from humility. Fasting brings you face-to-face with your limitations, but it also opens the door to a deeper reliance on God's grace and power. Embracing humility is not about diminishing yourself; it's about elevating God's role in your life and trusting Him to lift you up in His perfect timing.

As you continue your fast, remember that humility is a key to spiritual growth and intimacy with God. Trust that as you humble yourself before Him, He will exalt you in ways that align with His purpose for your life.

Each day of your fasting journey is a step closer to becoming the person God created you to be. As you cultivate humility, know that you are walking in the footsteps of Christ, who humbled Himself and was exalted by the Father.

> **LOOKING AHEAD: PREPARING FOR DAY 13**

Tomorrow, as you move into Day 13, the focus will shift to deepening your prayer life. Fasting and prayer are powerful partners, and as you progress in your fast, you'll explore how to enrich your prayer life, making it more intimate, focused, and aligned with God's will.

As you prepare for tomorrow, ask God to draw you closer to Him in prayer, open your heart to deeper communication with Him, and guide your words and thoughts as you seek His presence. Trust that He is with you, listening to your prayers and responding with love and wisdom.

CHAPTER 14

DAY 13

DEEPENING YOUR PRAYER LIFE

THE POWER OF PRAYER IN FASTING

Welcome to Day 13 of your fasting journey. As you've progressed through your fast, you may have noticed a growing intimacy with God, particularly in your prayer life. Fasting and prayer are inseparable partners—fasting without prayer is merely a physical exercise, but when combined with prayer, fasting becomes a powerful spiritual discipline that brings you closer to God. Today's focus is on deepening your prayer life, enhancing your ability to communicate with God, and aligning your prayers more closely with His will.

Prayer is the lifeline of the believer, a direct line of communication with the Creator of the universe. It's through prayer that we pour out our hearts to God, seek His guidance, and experience His presence. During fasting, your prayers become more focused and fervent, as the act of fasting heightens your spiritual sensitivity and your dependence on God. Today, you are invited to dive deeper into your prayer life, explore new dimensions of prayer, and experience the transformative power that comes from truly connecting with God.

This chapter will guide you in understanding the importance of deepening your prayer life during fasting, how to make your prayers more effective, and how prayer can transform your fasting experience.

> **OVERVIEW OF DAY 13:**
> **ENRICHING YOUR COMMUNION WITH GOD**

The theme for Day 13 is deepening your prayer life—a crucial aspect of your spiritual journey that involves not just talking to God but truly communing with Him. Prayer during fasting is different from everyday prayer; it's often more intense, more focused, and more transformational. Fasting strips away distractions, allowing you to focus more fully on God and to hear His voice more clearly.

Deepening your prayer life means moving beyond surface-level requests and entering into a deeper, more intimate conversation with God. It's about listening as much as speaking, seeking God's will as much as presenting your own needs, and opening your heart to His transformative power.

Today is about embracing the opportunity to deepen your prayer life, explore different forms of prayer, and make prayer the foundation of your fasting journey. As you do so, you'll find that prayer not only sustains you during fasting but also draws you into a closer, more intimate relationship with God.

> **SCRIPTURE OF THE DAY: PHILIPPIANS 4:6-7**

"Do not be anxious about anything, but in every situation, by prayer and petition, with thanksgiving, present your requests to God. And the peace of God, which transcends all understanding, will guard your hearts and your minds in Christ Jesus."—Philippians 4:6-7

Today's scripture from Philippians is a powerful reminder of the peace that comes from prayer. Paul encourages believers to bring everything to God in prayer, with a heart of thanksgiving, and to trust that God's peace will guard their hearts and minds.

As you meditate on this verse, consider how your prayers can be filled with both petitions and thanksgiving. Are there areas of your life where anxiety has crept in? How can you bring these concerns to God in prayer and experience His peace?

Prayer is not just about asking for things; it's about entering into God's presence with a heart of gratitude and trust. Today, let this verse guide you into a deeper, more peaceful prayer life, where you can release your anxieties and receive the peace that surpasses all understanding.

> **KEY THOUGHT:**
> **PRAYER IS THE ANCHOR OF FASTING.**

Today's key thought is that prayer is the anchor of fasting. Just as a ship needs an anchor to stay steady in the midst of a storm, your fasting journey needs the anchor of prayer to keep you grounded, focused, and connected to God. Without prayer, fasting can become a mere act of self-denial, but with prayer, it becomes a powerful spiritual practice that draws you closer to God.

Prayer during fasting is not just about presenting your needs to God; it's about deepening your relationship with Him, seeking His will, and aligning your heart with His. It's about spending time in His presence, listening for His voice, and allowing His Spirit to guide and transform you.

As you move through today, reflect on how prayer is anchoring your fasting journey. How is it helping you to stay focused on God? How is it deepening your relationship with Him? Embrace the power of prayer, knowing that it is the key to experiencing the fullness of God's presence and power during your fast.

> **PRAYER PROMPT:**
> **A PRAYER FOR DEEPER COMMUNION**

Today's prayer focus is on asking God to deepen your prayer life and to help you experience a more intimate communion with Him. This is an opportunity to ask for a heart that seeks after God, a mind that is attuned to His voice, and a spirit that is open to His leading.

PRAYER PROMPT:

"Father, I come to You today, longing for a deeper communion with You. I thank You for the gift of prayer, for the privilege of entering into Your presence and pouring out my heart to You. Lord, I ask that You would deepen my prayer life, that You would draw me closer to You, and that You would teach me to pray according to Your will. Help me to listen for Your voice, to seek Your guidance, and to align my heart with Yours. I surrender my anxieties, my fears, and my desires to You, trusting that You will fill me with Your peace. Lord, I want to know You more, to experience Your presence more fully, and to be transformed by Your Spirit. Thank You for hearing my prayers and for drawing me closer to You. In Jesus's name, I pray. Amen."

> ## SCIENTIFIC INSIGHT:
> ## EMOTIONAL AND COGNITIVE RESILIENCE

KEYWORD DEFINITION: EMOTIONAL AND COGNITIVE RESILIENCE

Emotional and cognitive resilience is your mind's ability to adapt and recover from challenges, maintaining a steady mental and emotional state even when faced with stress or setbacks. Emotional resilience helps you stay balanced and manage emotions effectively, while cognitive resilience enables you to think clearly, solve problems, and make decisions, even under pressure. Together, these qualities are like mental flexibility and strength, allowing you to navigate life's ups and downs without being easily overwhelmed. During fasting, emotional and cognitive resilience can be especially valuable, as they help you manage cravings, maintain focus, and adapt to the shifts your body and mind are experiencing.[25] The cited article speaks to the concept of resilience

Your body has adapted well to fasting, and you're now experiencing increased emotional and cognitive resilience. The ongoing autophagy and ketone production is doing wonders for your brain, keeping you sharp and emotionally steady.

THE NEUROSCIENCE OF PRAYER AND MEDITATION

Prayer, especially during fasting, is not just a spiritual exercise; it also has profound effects on the brain. Neuroscientific research has shown that prayer and meditation can lead to significant changes in brain structure and function, enhancing mental and emotional well-being.[26]

---

25 Gang Wu wt al., "Understanding resilience," *Frontiers in Behavioral Science* 7, no. 10 (2013): 1-15, https://doi.org/10.3389/fnbeh.2013.00010.
26 Felix Chin et al., "Efficacy of prayer in inducing immediate physiological changes: a systematic analysis of objective experiments," *Journal of Complementary and Integrative Medicine* 18, no. 4 (2021): 679-84, https://doi.org/10.1515/jcim-2020-0075.

Prayer, like meditation, engages specific regions of the brain, particularly the prefrontal cortex and the anterior cingulate cortex. The outcomes of the research found that prayer activity has objective outcomes on the human brain. Regular prayer and meditation can increase the thickness of the prefrontal cortex, leading to improved cognitive function, better emotional regulation, and enhanced self-control.[27]

During fasting, when the brain is already undergoing changes due to the altered metabolic state, prayer can enhance these effects, leading to greater mental clarity, focus, and spiritual sensitivity. This combination of fasting and prayer creates a powerful environment for spiritual growth and transformation.

As you continue your fast, remember that prayer is not only sustaining you spiritually but also enhancing your mental and emotional well-being. By deepening your prayer life during fasting, you are opening yourself to the transformative power of God, who is at work in every aspect of your being.

DAY 13 TIP: **HYDRATION FOR DETOX AND ENHANCED MENTAL CLARITY**

On Day 13 of your twenty-one-day fast, drinking water is essential as your body continues to detox deeply. Staying hydrated helps flush out toxins efficiently, supporting your kidneys and liver in this cleansing phase. Hydration is also crucial for maintaining mental clarity and focus, especially as your body's energy sources shift. Keep sipping water throughout the day, and if you need an extra boost, try adding a pinch of Himalayan salt for minerals that support hydration and balance. Each glass of water you drink today aids your body in its renewal process, keeping you clear-headed and energized.

---

[27] Eileen Luders et al., "The underlying anatomical correlates of long-term meditation: Larger hippocampal and frontal volumes of gray matter," *NeuroImage* 45, no.3: (2009): 672-78, https://doi.org/10.1016/j.neuroimage.2008.12.061.

JOURNALING: **REFLECTING ON PRAYER**

Journaling today provides an opportunity to reflect on the role of prayer in your fasting journey. Use this time to document your thoughts, prayers, and any insights you receive about how prayer is shaping your spiritual and emotional well-being.

JOURNALING PROMPTS:

1) How has your prayer life changed during this fast? Reflect on any specific ways your prayers have deepened or become more focused. How is God using this time of fasting to draw you closer to Him through prayer?

_____
_____
_____
_____
_____
_____
_____

2) What have you learned about the power of prayer? Consider the ways in which prayer has impacted your mental and emotional well-being during this fast. How is prayer helping you to maintain peace, focus, and resilience?

_____
_____

3) How does the scientific understanding of prayer enhance your spiritual practice? Think about how the brain's response to prayer aligns with the spiritual benefits of communing with God. How can you use this knowledge to deepen your prayer life during your fast?

4) What prayers are on your heart today? Write out a personal prayer expressing your desire to deepen your communion with God. Thank Him for the gift of prayer and ask for His continued guidance and presence in your life.

_____

_____

_____

_____

_____

Journaling helps you to capture the spiritual and emotional benefits of deepening your prayer life during your fast. It's a way to document your journey, reflect on the growth you're experiencing, and deepen your connection with God through prayer.

ENCOURAGEMENT FOR THE JOURNEY AHEAD

As you conclude Day 13, take a moment to recognize the profound impact that prayer is having on your fasting journey. Prayer is not just a routine practice; it's the anchor that holds you steady, the lifeline that connects you to God, and the key that unlocks the peace and power of His presence. As you deepen your prayer life, you are drawing closer to God, aligning your heart with His, and opening yourself to the transformative work He is doing in you.

As you continue your fast, let prayer be your constant companion, guiding your thoughts, calming your spirit, and drawing you ever closer to the heart of God. Trust that as you pray, God is listening, responding, and working in your life in ways that are far beyond what you can imagine.

Each day of your fasting journey is an opportunity to experience the power of prayer in a deeper, more transformative way. As you deepen your prayer life, know that you are building a foundation that will sustain you not only during this fast but in every aspect of your spiritual walk.

LOOKING AHEAD: **PREPARING FOR DAY 14**

Tomorrow, as you move into Day 14, the focus will be on the power of worship. Worship, like prayer, is a vital component of your spiritual journey, especially during fasting. On Day 14, you'll explore how worship can elevate your fasting experience, draw you into God's presence, and transform your heart.

As you prepare for tomorrow, ask God to open your heart to worship, fill you with a spirit of praise, and help you experience the joy of His presence in a new and profound way. Trust that He is with you, guiding you, and drawing you closer to Himself through every act of worship.

CHAPTER 15

DAY 14

ELEVATING YOUR WORSHIP

THE HEART OF WORSHIP

Welcome to Day 14 of your fasting journey. As you continue to draw nearer to God through fasting and prayer, another vital aspect of your spiritual life comes into focus: worship. Worship is more than just a ritual or a set of songs; it's an expression of your love, reverence, and adoration for God. Today's focus is on elevating your worship, allowing it to become a powerful force that draws you into deeper communion with God.

Worship is the natural response of a heart that is captivated by the greatness and goodness of God. It is an outpouring of praise and thanksgiving that acknowledges who God is and what He has done. During fasting, worship takes on a new depth, as the physical act of denying yourself food sharpens your spiritual senses and makes you more aware of God's presence.

This chapter will guide you in understanding the importance of worship during fasting, how to elevate your worship experience, and how worship can transform your heart and bring you closer to God.

OVERVIEW OF DAY 14: THE TRANSFORMATIVE POWER OF WORSHIP

The theme for Day 14 is elevating your worship—a practice that goes beyond words and music to become a lifestyle of devotion and surrender to God. Fasting is a time of stripping away distractions, and in this place of simplicity, worship can become more profound and heartfelt. When you worship during fasting, you are not only praising God with your lips but also with your entire being, as your fast becomes an offering of worship to Him.

Worship during fasting is not limited to singing; it encompasses every act of devotion, from prayer and meditation to acts of service and obedience. It's about turning your heart fully toward God, recognizing His sovereignty, and responding with awe and reverence.

Today is about embracing worship in its fullest sense, allowing it to permeate every aspect of your life during this fast. As you do so, you'll find that worship not only elevates your spirit but also brings you into a deeper, more intimate relationship with God.

SCRIPTURE OF THE DAY: PSALM 29:2

"Ascribe to the LORD the glory due his name; worship the LORD in the splendor of his holiness."—Psalm 29:2

Today's scripture from Psalm 29 calls us to ascribe to the Lord the glory due His name and to worship Him in the splendor of His holiness. This verse is a reminder that worship is not about us; it's about giving God the honor and glory He deserves.

As you meditate on this verse, consider how you can ascribe glory to God in your own life. What aspects of His character and works inspire your worship today? How can you worship Him in the splendor of His holiness, recognizing His majesty and greatness?

Worship is an invitation to enter into the presence of God, behold His beauty, and respond with reverence and adoration. Today, let this verse inspire you to elevate your worship, focus on God's holiness, and offer Him the glory that is due His name.

> **KEY THOUGHT:**
> **WORSHIP IS A RESPONSE TO GOD'S GREATNESS.**

Today's key thought is that worship is a response to God's greatness. True worship flows from a heart that is deeply moved by the majesty, power, and goodness of God. It is not something we do out of obligation, but out of a genuine recognition of who God is and what He has done in our lives.

Fasting creates a space where this recognition can grow and deepen. As you fast, you become more aware of your dependence on God, more attuned to His presence, and more grateful for His provision. This heightened awareness naturally leads to worship—a response that honors God and draws you closer to Him.

As you move through today, reflect on how worship is shaping your fasting journey. How is it helping you to see God more clearly and to respond with a heart full of praise and gratitude? Embrace the power of worship, knowing that it is a gateway to experiencing the fullness of God's presence.

> **PRAYER PROMPT: A PRAYER OF ADORATION**

Today's prayer focus is on offering a prayer of adoration, expressing your love, reverence, and awe for God. This is an opportunity to lift your heart in worship, focus on God's greatness, and declare His worthiness.

PRAYER PROMPT:

"Lord, I come before You today with a heart full of adoration. I worship You for who You are—the Creator of all things, the King of kings, and the Lord of lords. You are holy, righteous, and just, yet full of mercy, grace, and love. I ascribe to You the glory due Your name, recognizing that You alone are worthy of all praise. Lord, in the splendor of Your holiness, I bow before You in awe and reverence. I thank You for Your goodness, for Your faithfulness, and for the countless ways You have shown Your love to me. Help me to worship You not only with my lips but with my whole life, offering everything I am as a living sacrifice of praise. May my worship be pleasing to You, and may it draw me ever closer to Your heart. In Jesus's name, I pray. Amen."

> **SCIENTIFIC INSIGHT: STRENGTH AND ENDURANCE**

KEYWORD DEFINITION: ENDURANCE

Endurance is the body's ability to sustain prolonged physical or mental activity without exhaustion. It's like a battery that, over time, learns to last longer and perform better, even under challenging conditions. In the body, endurance depends on the efficiency of energy use, cardiovascular health, and muscle resilience. During fasting, building endurance—both physically and mentally—helps you maintain steady energy, focus, and resilience. As your body adapts to fasting, it becomes better at conserving and utilizing energy, enhancing your overall stamina and resilience.[28]

Your physical endurance is improving, and muscle preservation is supported by elevated growth hormone levels. You should feel a notable increase in strength, both physically and spiritually.

This far into your fast, your body has made remarkable adaptations to support endurance. Initially, you relied on glycogen stores for energy, but now, as these reserves are long depleted, your body has fully shifted to burning fat, entering a sustained state of ketosis. This change trains your body to be more efficient with energy, as it taps into fat stores to keep you going. During this period, mitochondrial biogenesis—where new energy-producing mitochondria are formed—kicks in, helping each cell generate energy more effectively. This increased efficiency boosts your overall stamina and resilience. Additionally, fasting can reduce inflammation and improve mental clarity, strengthening both physical and mental endurance. By Day 14, your body is not only fueling itself differently but also becoming more adept at sustaining prolonged activity, focus, and stability. Each day of fasting has built up your body's endurance, making it better equipped to handle extended periods of energy demand with ease.

> **DAY 14 TIP: WATER FOR ENHANCED FAT METABOLISM AND ENERGY**

On Day 14 of your twenty-one-day fast, hydration is essential as your body continues to burn fat for fuel. Drinking water helps optimize this fat

---

[28] Michael J. Joyner and Edward F. Coyle, "Endurance exercise performance: the physiology of champions," *The Journal of Physiology* 586, no. 1 (2008): 35-44, ttps://doi.org/10.1113/jphysiol.2007.143834.

metabolism process, supporting the breakdown and elimination of byproducts that can build up as your body relies on fat stores for energy. Staying hydrated also helps maintain mental clarity and supports your endurance, especially as your body works harder to sustain itself. Make sure to drink water regularly throughout the day—consider adding a slice of lemon for flavor and an added boost of antioxidants. Keeping hydrated today will maximize your body's efficiency, helping you feel energized and focused as you reach this powerful stage of your fast!

JOURNALING: REFLECTING ON WORSHIP

Journaling today provides an opportunity to reflect on the role of worship in your fasting journey. Use this time to document your thoughts, prayers, and any insights you receive about how worship is shaping your spiritual and emotional well-being.

JOURNALING PROMPTS:

1) How has worship influenced your fasting experience? Reflect on the ways that worship has deepened your connection with God during this fast. How has it changed your perspective or brought you closer to Him?

___
___
___
___
___
___

2) What aspects of God's character inspire your worship? Consider the attributes of God that most move you to worship. How do these qualities influence your relationship with Him and your approach to fasting?

___

3) How does the scientific understanding of worship enhance your spiritual practice? Think about how the brain's response to worship aligns with the spiritual benefits of praising God. How can you use this knowledge to elevate your worship during your fast?

___

4) What prayers of adoration are on your heart today? Write out a personal prayer expressing your adoration for God. Focus on His greatness, His holiness, and His love, and offer your worship as a sacrifice of praise.

_____
_____
_____
_____
_____
_____
_____

Journaling helps you to capture the spiritual and emotional benefits of worship during your fast. It's a way to document your journey, reflect on the growth you're experiencing, and deepen your connection with God through praise and adoration.

ENCOURAGEMENT FOR THE JOURNEY AHEAD

As you conclude Day 14, take a moment to recognize the transformative power of worship in your fasting journey. Worship is more than just a practice; it's an encounter with the living God, a response to His majesty and love, and a doorway to deeper intimacy with Him. As you elevate your worship, you are not only praising God for who He is but also inviting His presence to fill your life in new and powerful ways.

As you continue your fast, let worship be the breath of your spirit, the song of your heart, and the focus of your mind. Trust that as you worship, God is drawing you closer, revealing more of Himself, and transforming you into His likeness.

Each day of your fasting journey is an opportunity to experience the power of worship in a deeper, more profound way. As you elevate your worship, know that you are stepping into the presence of God, where you will find joy, peace, and transformation beyond measure.

> **LOOKING AHEAD: PREPARING FOR DAY 15**

Tomorrow, as you move into Day 15, the focus will shift to the theme of intercession. Fasting often brings a heightened sense of spiritual awareness, making it an ideal time to pray for others and stand in the gap on their behalf. On Day 15, you'll explore how intercession can deepen your prayer life, strengthen your community, and align your heart with God's purposes.

As you prepare for tomorrow, ask God to guide your prayers, open your heart to the needs of others, and use you as a vessel of His love and power through intercession. Trust that He is with you, leading you, and empowering you to make a difference through your prayers.

CHAPTER 16

DAY 15

THE POWER OF INTERCESSION

STANDING IN THE GAP

Welcome to Day 15 of your fasting journey. You've come a long way, and as you continue to press deeper into this spiritual walk through fasting, prayer, and worship, another crucial element of your faith journey comes into focus: **intercession.**

Intercession is more than just prayer—it's the powerful act of standing in the gap for others, bringing their needs, struggles, and hopes before God with compassion and faith. Today, we will explore how your prayers, especially during this time of fasting, can have a profound impact on the lives of others.

When you intercede, you step into a place of selfless love and devotion, choosing to carry the burdens of others to the Lord. It's a beautiful expression of faith, trusting in God's power to heal, restore, and provide—not just for you but for those you care about, and even for those you may not know personally. During a fast, your spiritual sensitivity is heightened and your heart more attuned to the whispers of the Holy Spirit, making it an ideal time to intercede with greater passion and focus.

Fasting amplifies the effectiveness of your intercession. It strips away distractions, sharpens your spiritual focus, and aligns your heart more closely with God's purposes. As you sacrifice physical nourishment, you become a conduit through which God's power can flow more freely, not just for your own life, but for the lives of those you are praying for.

This chapter is designed to guide you in understanding the immense importance of intercession during fasting. You'll learn how to approach it with a heart full of compassion, faith, and fervor. As you stand in the gap for others, know that your prayers are a powerful force, capable of bringing transformation, healing, and breakthrough in ways that go beyond human understanding.

Today, let your fasting and prayers become a bridge between heaven and earth, where the needs of others are met by the unlimited grace and power of God.

OVERVIEW OF DAY 15: THE MINISTRY OF INTERCESSION

The theme for Day 15 is the power of intercession—a ministry that every believer is called to participate in. Intercession is more than just praying for others; it is a partnership with God, where you stand in the gap on behalf of those in need, seeking His intervention in their lives. Fasting enhances this ministry by deepening your spiritual insight and aligning your prayers more closely with God's will.

Intercession requires empathy, perseverance, and faith. It involves listening to the Holy Spirit, discerning the needs of others, and bringing those needs before God with confidence that He hears and answers prayers. As you fast, your spirit is more attuned to the voice of God and the needs of those around you, making your intercessory prayers more effective and impactful.

Today is about embracing the ministry of intercession, allowing your prayers to become a channel of God's love and power in the lives of others. As you do so, you'll find that intercession not only blesses those you pray for but also deepens your relationship with God and strengthens your own faith.

> **SCRIPTURE OF THE DAY: 1 TIMOTHY 2:1**

"I urge, then, first of all, that petitions, prayers, intercession and thanksgiving be made for all people."—1 Timothy 2:1

Today's scripture from 1 Timothy highlights the importance of making intercession a priority in your prayer life. Paul urges believers to pray for all people, emphasizing the need for petitions, intercessions, and thanksgiving on behalf of others.

As you meditate on this verse, consider how you can incorporate intercession into your daily prayers. Who are the people in your life who need your prayers today? How can you bring their needs before God with faith and compassion?

Intercession is a powerful way to serve others and participate in God's work in the world. Today, let this verse inspire you to make intercession a regular part of your prayer life, trusting that your prayers can make a difference in the lives of those you lift up before God.

> **KEY THOUGHT:**
> **INTERCESSION AMPLIFIES COMPASSION.**

Today's key thought is that intercession amplifies compassion. When you intercede for others, you are stepping into their shoes, sharing in their burdens, and bringing their needs before God with a heart of love and empathy. Fasting enhances this process by softening your heart, increasing your sensitivity to the needs of others, and aligning your prayers more closely with the heart of God.

Intercession is an act of selflessness, where you set aside your own needs to focus on the needs of others. It is a powerful way to demonstrate God's love, as you become a vessel through which His grace, healing, and provision can flow. As you fast, your capacity for compassion deepens, making your intercessory prayers more heartfelt and effective.

As you move through today, reflect on how intercession is shaping your fasting journey. How is it helping you to develop a greater sense of empathy and compassion for others? How is it drawing you closer to the heart of God? Embrace the power of intercession, knowing that it is a vital part of your spiritual life and a powerful tool for making a difference in the world.

> PRAYER PROMPT: **A PRAYER FOR OTHERS**

Today's prayer focus is on interceding for others—bringing their needs, struggles, and desires before God with faith and compassion. This is an opportunity to lift up those who are in need, stand in the gap on their behalf, and ask for God's intervention in their lives.

PRAYER PROMPT:

"Father, I come to You today with a heart full of compassion for those in need. I lift up [specific names or groups] before You, asking for Your healing, provision, and guidance in their lives. Lord, I intercede on their behalf, standing in the gap and bringing their needs before Your throne of grace. I ask that You would move in their lives in powerful ways, that You would bring comfort to those who are hurting, peace to those who are anxious, and provision to those who are in need. Lord, give me the wisdom to pray according to Your will and the faith to trust

that You hear and answer my prayers. Thank You for the privilege of interceding for others, and for the ways You are working in their lives through my prayers. In Jesus's name, I pray. Amen."

SCIENTIFIC INSIGHT: ENHANCED CELLULAR LONGEVITY

KEYWORD DEFINITION: CELLULAR LONGEVITY

Cellular longevity refers to the lifespan and health of individual cells, which play a key role in overall aging and vitality. It's like each cell having a "life clock" that can be slowed down or sped up depending on factors like diet, stress, and cellular repair processes. During fasting, cellular longevity is supported by processes like autophagy, where damaged cell parts are broken down and recycled, allowing cells to function more efficiently and stay healthier for longer. Additionally, fasting can activate pathways that protect against cellular damage and reduce oxidative stress, both of which are essential for cellular longevity. This cellular renewal ultimately supports your body's resilience and longevity, helping slow the effects of aging.[29]

Today, your body is optimizing for long-term health. Autophagy is reducing the risk of chronic diseases by clearing out old cells and generating new ones. Your metabolism is running efficiently, burning fat for sustained energy.

Your body is now fully engaged in promoting cellular longevity, keeping your cells youthful and resilient. This is a transformative stage where, without the demands of digestion, your body shifts focus to cellular repair and renewal. One of the key processes at play is autophagy—a "self-cleaning" process where cells identify and recycle old, damaged parts. This internal cleanup helps

---

[29] Juan José Carmona and Shaday Michan, "Biology of Healthy Aging and Longevity," Revista de Investigación Clínica 68, no. 1 (2016): 7-16.

prevent the buildup of waste, allowing cells to function more efficiently, much like decluttering your home creates a more organized space.

Additionally, fasting at this stage helps reduce oxidative stress, a type of cellular "wear and tear" that contributes to aging. By enhancing the body's antioxidant defenses, fasting minimizes this damage, allowing cells to stay healthier for longer. This combined action of autophagy and reduced oxidative stress promotes cellular health, supporting your body's resilience and longevity.

As you continue through Day 15, it's not just about reaching the end of your fast; your body is actively working to renew and strengthen itself from within, laying the foundation for a healthier, more vibrant life. Each sip of water and each moment you spend fasting is contributing to this deep cellular renewal, setting the stage for long-term health benefits.

Intercession and Emotional Resilience

While cellular longevity is happening, remain in a prayerful state of intercession, remembering that fasting without praying is just a hunger strike. Intercession has also been shown to increase emotional resilience. When you pray for others, you are not only helping them but also reinforcing your own ability to cope with stress and adversity. One study found that individuals who engage in intercessory prayer exhibit greater emotional resilience, better coping strategies, and a stronger sense of purpose.[30]

This increased resilience comes from the practice of shifting your focus from your own challenges to the needs of others, which can provide perspective and reduce the impact of personal stress. Fasting, when combined with intercession, further enhances this resilience by deepening your spiritual connection and reliance on God.

As you continue your fast, remember that intercession is not just an act of compassion but also a powerful tool for spiritual growth. By interceding for

---

[30] Antonius Skipper et al., "'The prayers of others helped': Intercessory prayer as a source of coping and resilience in Christian African American families," *Journal of Religion & Spirituality in Social Work* 37, no.4 (2018): 373-94, https://doi.org/10.1080/15426432.2018.1500970.

others, you are participating in God's work in the world, deepening your own faith, and experiencing the transformative power of prayer.

> **DAY 15 TIP: WATER FOR DEEP CELLULAR RENEWAL AND DETOXIFICATION**

On Day 15 of your twenty-one-day fast, your body is in a powerful phase of cellular renewal, and hydration is essential to support this process. Drinking water helps flush out toxins and waste products that are released as your cells undergo repair and recycling. Proper hydration also sustains your energy and mental clarity, especially as your body continues to adapt and dig deeper into the fast. Aim to drink water steadily throughout the day and consider herbal teas for a change. Each sip aids your body's cellular renewal, helping you maximize the restorative benefits of your fast.

> **JOURNALING: REFLECTING ON INTERCESSION**

Journaling today provides an opportunity to reflect on the role of intercession in your fasting journey. Use this time to document your thoughts, prayers, and any insights you receive about how intercession is shaping your spiritual and emotional well-being.

JOURNALING PROMPTS:

1) Who are you interceding for today? Reflect on the specific people or groups that God has placed on your heart to pray for. How are you bringing their needs before God in prayer?

_____

_____

2) How is intercession impacting your spiritual growth? Consider how praying for others is deepening your faith, increasing your empathy, and drawing you closer to God. How is intercession transforming your relationship with God and others?

3) How does the scientific understanding of intercession enhance your spiritual practice? Think about how the psychological benefits of empathy and resilience align with the spiritual practice of interceding for others. How can you use this knowledge to deepen your intercessory prayers during your fast?

4) What prayers of intercession are on your heart today? Write out a personal prayer interceding for those in need, asking for God's intervention, healing, and provision in their lives. Express your trust in His power to answer your prayers and to bring about His will.

Journaling helps you to capture the spiritual and emotional benefits of intercession during your fast. It's a way to document your journey, reflect on the growth you're experiencing, and deepen your connection with God and others through prayer.

ENCOURAGEMENT FOR THE JOURNEY AHEAD

As you conclude Day 15, take a moment to recognize the power and privilege of intercession in your fasting journey. Interceding for others is more than an act of compassion—it is a way for you to actively participate in God's ongoing work in the world. Through your prayers, you have the incredible opportunity to invite healing, comfort, and provision into the lives of others, and to experience the joy of watching God move in response to your intercession.

As you continue your fast, let intercession become a cornerstone of your prayer life. It's an expression of love for others and trust in God's power to intervene. Every time you stand in the gap for someone, believe that God is working—both in their life and in yours—bringing about His perfect will and revealing His boundless love.

Each day of this fasting journey is an invitation to deepen your intercession. The act of praying for others holds transformative power, not only for them but for you. As you continue to stand in the gap, trust that your prayers are making a difference. You are part of something greater, part of God's purpose to bring hope, healing, and restoration into the world.

LOOKING AHEAD: **PREPARING FOR DAY 16**

Tomorrow, as you move into Day 16, the focus will shift to the theme of surrender. Fasting is an act of surrender, where you lay down your desires and submit your will to God. On Day 16, you'll explore how surrendering to God's will can lead to greater freedom, peace, and alignment with His purposes.

As you prepare for tomorrow, ask God to give you the strength to surrender fully to Him, trust in His plans, and find peace in His sovereignty. Trust that He is with you, guiding you, and leading you into a deeper experience of His love and grace.

CHAPTER 17

DAY 16

THE FREEDOM OF SURRENDER

THE BEAUTY OF LETTING GO

Welcome to Day 16 of your fasting journey. Today, we turn our attention to one of the most profound themes you will encounter during fasting: **surrender**. Surrender is not a sign of weakness or defeat—it's a choice, an intentional act of laying down your own will and fully trusting in God's greater plan for your life. Today's focus is on the freedom that comes with surrender—how releasing your grip on life's outcomes can lead to a deeper sense of peace, alignment with God's will, and spiritual growth.

Surrender is an act of faith and trust. It's a conscious decision to place your life, your desires, and your future into God's hands, knowing that He sees the bigger picture and holds your best interest at heart. During a fast, this act of surrender takes on even more significance. The physical abstinence from food is a powerful symbol of spiritual surrender—releasing control and trusting in God's strength to carry you.

As you fast today, allow yourself to let go of your fears, anxieties, and ambitions. This is your time to embrace the peace that comes from surrendering to God's sovereignty, trusting that He is in control. When you surrender, you open the door to deeper faith, spiritual maturity, and a closeness with God that can only be experienced when you release control.

> ### OVERVIEW OF DAY 16:
> ### THE LIBERATING POWER OF SURRENDER

The theme for today is the **liberating power of surrender**—how letting go of your will and submitting to God's authority can bring true freedom and peace. Fasting is a practice that naturally leads us to surrender. It requires you to deny your physical desires and trust in God to provide the strength and sustenance you need.

But here's the beauty: surrender is not about giving up; it's about giving over. It's recognizing that you are not the ultimate authority in your life. True freedom comes when you submit to the One who knows you intimately, created you with love, and holds your future in His hands. Fasting invites you to loosen your grip on the things you cannot control and trust that God's plans are good and perfect.

Today is about embracing the freedom that comes with surrender—allowing God to take the lead, trusting Him with your heart, and experiencing the peace that surpasses all understanding. As you surrender your will to God, you'll discover that surrender is not a burden. It's a gift, a liberating invitation to rest in God's loving care and to draw closer to His heart.

> ### SCRIPTURE OF THE DAY: **MATTHEW 16:24-25**

"Then Jesus said to his disciples, 'Whoever wants to be my disciple must deny themselves and take up their cross and follow me. For whoever

wants to save their life will lose it, but whoever loses their life for me will find it.'"—Matthew 16:24-25

Today's scripture from Matthew emphasizes the call to surrender—denying yourself, taking up your cross, and following Jesus. This passage highlights the paradox of surrender: in losing your life, you find it; in letting go, you gain.

As you meditate on this verse, consider what it means to deny yourself and take up your cross. Are there areas of your life where you are struggling to let God take the reins of your life? How can you surrender these areas to God and trust Him to lead you?

Surrender is not an act of weakness but an act of strength, as it requires courage to let go and faith to trust in God's plan. Today, let this verse challenge you to embrace surrender, knowing that in doing so, you will discover the true life that God has for you.

> **KEY THOUGHT: SURRENDER LEADS TO FREEDOM.**

Today's key thought is that surrender leads to freedom. When you let go of your need to control every aspect of your life and surrender to God's will, you experience a freedom that cannot be found in striving or self-reliance. Fasting is a powerful way to practice this surrender, as it requires you to trust in God's provision and to release your hold on physical and spiritual cravings.

Surrender is about recognizing that you are not in charge, and that's okay. It's about finding peace in the knowledge that God is sovereign, and His plans are higher and better than anything you could imagine. As you fast, you are practicing the art of surrender, learning to let go of your desires and trust in God's perfect timing and provision.

As you move through today, reflect on how surrender is shaping your fasting journey. How is it helping you to release control and to experience the freedom that comes from trusting in God? Embrace the power of surrender, knowing that it is the pathway to true spiritual freedom and peace.

> ### PRAYER PROMPT: A PRAYER OF SURRENDER

Today's prayer focus is on surrendering your life, your desires, and your will to God. This is an opportunity to release control, trust in God's plan, and embrace the freedom that comes from letting go.

PRAYER PROMPT:

"Lord, I come to You today with a heart that is ready to surrender. I acknowledge that I often try to control my life, my circumstances, and my future, but I know that true freedom comes from surrendering to You. Lord, I lay down my fears, my anxieties, and my desires at Your feet, trusting that Your plans for me are good. Help me to let go of my need to control and instead embrace the peace that comes from trusting in Your sovereignty. Teach me to deny myself, to take up my cross, and to follow You with a heart that is fully surrendered. Thank You for the freedom that comes from letting go and for the life that I find in You. In Jesus's name, I pray. Amen."

> ### SCIENTIFIC INSIGHT: INCREASED DETOXIFICATION AND MENTAL CLARITY

KEYWORD DEFINITION: MENTAL CLARITY

Mental clarity is the state of having a clear, focused, and organized mind, allowing you to think efficiently and make decisions with ease. Scientifically, mental clarity is linked to the brain's energy supply, neurotransmitter balance, and overall brain health. During fasting, many people report heightened mental clarity because the body shifts its energy source to ketones, which can provide a steady and efficient fuel for the brain. This change in energy can help reduce brain fog and enhance focus, giving a feeling of mental sharpness. Mental clarity also benefits from the reduction of oxidative stress and inflammation in the brain, both of which fasting can help minimize.[31]

Your body continues to detoxify, eliminating any remaining toxins at a cellular level. Your mental clarity is likely at an all-time high, as your brain thrives on the steady supply of ketones.

The body has become adept at using ketones as its primary fuel source, which can lead to a profound sense of mental clarity. Ketones provide a steady and efficient energy supply to the brain, often resulting in a heightened ability to focus, clearer thinking, and a reduction in the mental fog that may have been present earlier. This shift in energy source supports not only cognitive sharpness but also a calm, sustained focus that many fasters describe as a "mental high." At this point, fasting also helps reduce oxidative stress and inflammation in the brain, allowing neurons to function more effectively and improving the overall environment for cognitive processes.

This clarity isn't just about sharper thinking—it also impacts how you experience each moment. You may find that tasks feel more manageable, decisions come more easily, and your thoughts feel organized. Many people describe this state as a refreshing "reset" for the mind, a break from the usual cluttered thinking patterns. As you progress through Day 16, embrace this phase of mental clarity as one of fasting's key benefits, allowing you to focus deeply, make intentional choices, and connect more meaningfully with your inner thoughts and goals. This cognitive clarity is a powerful gift from your body, showing you how a change in energy sources can enhance not only physical

---

31 Benjamin Koch, "The Pathway to Mental Clarity: A Comprehensive Framework for Psychological and Ethical Well-being," unpublished manuscript, June 2024.

health but also mental resilience and awareness. The mental clarity you experience makes it easier to surrender to the process you are going through.

The Psychological Benefits of Surrender

Surrender, while primarily a spiritual practice, also has significant psychological benefits. Research in psychology has shown that the act of letting go—whether of control, anxiety, or unrealistic expectations—can lead to improved mental health, increased resilience, and greater overall well-being.

The Role of Letting Go in Emotional Health

Letting go of the need to control every aspect of your life can significantly reduce stress and anxiety. A study published in *Journal of Personality and Social Psychology Bulletin* found that individuals who practice psychological flexibility, including the ability to let go of control and accept uncertainty, experience lower levels of stress and higher levels of emotional well-being.[32] This aligns with the spiritual practice of surrender, where letting go is seen as a pathway to peace and freedom.

Surrendering to God's will, especially during fasting, can create a sense of relief and release, as you are no longer burdened by the need to manage every outcome. This release can lead to greater emotional stability, resilience in the face of challenges, and a deeper sense of peace.

By surrendering to God's will and trusting in His plan, you are building resilience, both spiritually and psychologically. This resilience allows you to navigate the ups and downs of life with greater grace and confidence, knowing that you are held by a loving and sovereign God.

As you continue your fast, remember that surrender is not a sign of defeat but a pathway to freedom and growth. By letting go of your own desires and trusting in God's plan, you are opening yourself to the transformative work of the Holy Spirit, who will lead you into greater freedom and peace.

---

32   Carver et al., "Assessing Coping Strategies: A Theoretically Based Approach," *Journal of Personality and Social Psychology* 56, no. 2 (1989): 267-83.

DAY 16 TIP: HYDRATION TO SUPPORT MENTAL CLARITY AND FOCUS

On Day 16 of your twenty-one-day fast, drinking water is essential to maintain the mental clarity you've gained. Staying hydrated helps keep your brain functioning at its best, supporting the enhanced focus and cognitive sharpness many people experience at this stage of fasting. Proper hydration also aids in flushing out any remaining toxins, allowing your body and mind to stay refreshed. Keep a water bottle nearby and sip regularly throughout the day—this simple habit will help you fully embrace the clear, focused state that comes with fasting, allowing you to feel present and energized as you continue your journey.

JOURNALING: REFLECTING ON SURRENDER

Journaling today provides an opportunity to reflect on the role of surrender in your fasting journey. Use this time to document your thoughts, prayers, and any insights you receive about how surrender is shaping your spiritual and emotional well-being.

JOURNALING PROMPTS:

1) What areas of your life are you surrendering to God today? Reflect on the specific aspects of your life where you feel called to let go of control. How are you trusting God to lead you in these areas?

_____

_____

_____

2) How is surrender bringing freedom and peace to your fasting journey? Consider how letting go of your own desires and submitting to God's will is impacting your emotional and spiritual well-being. How is surrender helping you to experience greater freedom and peace?

3) How does the scientific understanding of surrender enhance your spiritual practice? Think about how the psychological benefits of letting go align with the spiritual practice of surrender. How can you use this knowledge to deepen your surrender during your fast?

4) What prayers of surrender are on your heart today? Write out a personal prayer expressing your desire to surrender to God's will. Release your fears, anxieties, and desires, and ask for the freedom and peace that comes from trusting in His plan.

Journaling helps you to capture the spiritual and emotional benefits of surrender during your fast. It's a way to document your journey, reflect on the growth you're experiencing, and deepen your connection with God through the practice of letting go.

ENCOURAGEMENT FOR THE JOURNEY AHEAD

As you conclude Day 16, take a moment to embrace the freedom and peace that surrender brings into your fasting journey. Surrender isn't about giving up; it's about giving over—placing your life into the hands of a loving and sovereign God who knows what is best for you. By letting go of the need to control and submitting to God's will, you're opening yourself to a life of true freedom, peace, and profound spiritual growth.

As you continue your fast, let surrender become your daily practice. Release your anxieties and let the peace of trusting God's plan fill your heart. Trust that in your surrender, God is at work in ways you may not yet see—guiding you, protecting you, and leading you toward the fullness of His purposes.

Each day of your fasting journey is an invitation to experience the liberating power of surrender. With every moment you let go and trust in God, you are stepping deeper into a life of greater freedom, peace, and alignment with His will.

LOOKING AHEAD: PREPARING FOR DAY 17

Tomorrow, as you move into Day 17, the focus will shift to the theme of listening to God's voice. Fasting heightens your spiritual sensitivity, making it an ideal time to listen for God's guidance and direction. On Day 17, you'll explore how to cultivate a heart that is attuned to God's voice, and how to respond to His leading with faith and obedience.

As you prepare for tomorrow, ask God to open your ears to His voice, speak clearly to your heart, and guide you in every area of your life. Trust that He is with you, speaking to you, and leading you as you continue your fasting journey.

CHAPTER 18

DAY 17

ATTUNING TO GOD'S VOICE

THE ART OF LISTENING

Welcome to Day 17 of your fasting journey. As you've moved deeper into this fast, one of the most profound and rewarding aspects is the ability to hear God's voice with greater clarity. Fasting has a way of sharpening your spiritual sensitivity, allowing space for God to speak into your life in ways that are often drowned out by the noise of daily living. Today's focus is on attuning your heart and mind to His voice—learning to listen with intention and responding in faith.

Listening to God is an art, one that takes practice, patience, and a quieted soul. In the stillness that fasting brings, you'll find that you are more able to discern the gentle whispers of the Holy Spirit, guiding you, comforting you, and revealing God's will for your life. This chapter will help you cultivate the ability to hear God's voice more clearly, recognize His leading, and respond with trust and obedience.

> ## OVERVIEW OF DAY 17:
> ## CULTIVATING A LISTENING HEART

The theme for Day 17 is cultivating a listening heart—a heart that is open, attentive, and responsive to the voice of God. Fasting naturally quiets the noise of life, making it easier to hear God's still, small voice. However, listening to God is more than just a passive activity; it requires a deliberate effort to tune out distractions and to focus on His presence.

A listening heart is one that seeks God's guidance above all else, one that is eager to hear His voice and willing to follow His lead. As you fast, you are invited to slow down, create space in your heart and mind for God to speak, and embrace the quiet moments where His voice becomes clear.

Today is about developing the discipline of listening—of being still before God, of tuning in to the subtle ways He communicates, and of responding with a heart of obedience. As you do so, you'll find that listening to God not only brings clarity and direction but also deepens your relationship with Him.

> ## SCRIPTURE OF THE DAY: **1 KINGS 19:11-12**

"The LORD said, 'Go out and stand on the mountain in the presence of the LORD, for the LORD is about to pass by.' Then a great and powerful wind tore the mountains apart and shattered the rocks before the LORD, but the LORD was not in the wind. After the wind there was an earthquake, but the LORD was not in the earthquake. After the earthquake came a fire, but the LORD was not in the fire. And after the fire came a gentle whisper."—1 Kings 19:11-12

Today's scripture from 1 Kings recounts the story of Elijah on Mount Horeb, where he encounters God not in the wind, the earthquake, or the fire, but in a gentle whisper. This passage reminds us that God often speaks in the quiet moments, in ways that require us to be still and listen carefully.

As you meditate on this verse, consider how God might be speaking to you in the quiet moments of your fast. Are there areas of your life where you need His guidance? How can you create space to hear His gentle whisper?

Listening to God requires sensitivity and attentiveness. Today, let this verse inspire you to seek out the quiet places where you can hear God's voice, tune out the distractions, and be open to the subtle ways He communicates.

> **KEY THOUGHT:**
> **GOD'S VOICE IS FOUND IN THE STILLNESS.**

Today's key thought is that God's voice is often found in the stillness. In a world full of noise and busyness, it can be easy to miss the gentle whispers of the Holy Spirit. Fasting provides an opportunity to quiet your soul, step away from distractions, and focus on hearing God's voice.

God's voice is not always loud or dramatic; it often comes in the form of a gentle nudge, a quiet thought, or a deep sense of peace. As you fast, you are training your heart and mind to recognize these subtle cues, be attentive to the ways God is speaking to you, and respond with faith.

As you move through today, reflect on how stillness is helping you to hear God's voice more clearly. How is fasting creating space for you to listen? How can you cultivate a heart that is always tuned to the gentle whispers of God?

PRAYER PROMPT: A PRAYER FOR LISTENING

Today's prayer focus is on asking God to help you develop a listening heart. This is an opportunity to quiet your mind, focus on God's presence, and ask for the ability to hear His voice clearly and consistently.

PRAYER PROMPT:

"Lord, I come before You today with a desire to hear Your voice. I know that You are always speaking, but I confess that I am often too distracted to listen. Lord, I ask that You would quiet my mind, still my heart, and help me to tune in to Your gentle whispers. Teach me to recognize the subtle ways You communicate and give me the patience to wait in the stillness for Your guidance. Lord, I want to hear from You, to know Your will, and to follow Your leading. Help me to develop a listening heart, one that is always attuned to Your voice. Thank You for speaking to me, for guiding me, and for being present in every moment. In Jesus's name, I pray. Amen."

SCIENTIFIC INSIGHT: OPTIMIZED BRAIN FUNCTION AND EMOTIONAL STABILITY

KEYWORD DEFINITION: EMOTIONAL STABILITY

Emotional stability is the ability to stay calm, balanced, and resilient in the face of stress or changing circumstances. It's like having a steady anchor that keeps you grounded, even when emotions fluctuate. Scientifically, emotional stability is supported by balanced neurotransmitter activity, healthy stress response systems, and a well-regulated prefrontal cortex (the part of the brain responsible for decision-making and impulse control). During fasting, many people report experiencing increased emotional stability as the body reduces stress hormones and enhances mental clarity, both of which can help improve mood regulation and resilience.[33]

Today, your brain is operating at its best, with ketones fueling it efficiently. Emotionally, you're feeling balanced and at peace, as your body has fully adjusted to fasting.

One of the key observations you may find is that emotional stability has become one of the more unexpected yet powerful benefits of this journey. As your body has adapted to fasting, stress hormones like cortisol are often more balanced, creating a calmer, more centered emotional state. Additionally, the mental clarity from ketone use in the brain supports mood regulation, making it easier to maintain a balanced outlook and respond thoughtfully rather than reactively. Emotional stability on Day 17 feels like a steady calm—a foundation of resilience that allows you to handle challenges and stressors with a clearer, more grounded perspective. This sense of emotional balance is often accompanied by a deeper sense of gratitude and self-awareness, as fasting provides both physical and mental space to connect with your inner self. By embracing this phase of emotional stability, you can fully appreciate the emotional and spiritual depth that fasting can bring, helping you navigate life's highs and lows with greater calm and grace.

THE COGNITIVE BENEFITS OF MINDFULNESS AND LISTENING

Over and above emotional stability, listening, particularly in a spiritual context, is closely related to mindfulness—the practice of being fully present and attentive in the moment. Mindfulness can have significant cognitive and

---

33 Peter Hills and Michael Argyle, "Emotional stability as a major dimension of happiness," *Personality and Individual Differences* 31, no. 8 (2001): 1357-64, https://doi.org/10.1016/S0191-8869(00)00229-4.

emotional benefits, including improved focus, better emotional regulation, and enhanced mental clarity.

The Spiritual Impact of Listening During Fasting

Listening to God during fasting can lead to profound spiritual transformation. Individuals who engage in practices that enhance spiritual listening, such as fasting and prayer, experience deeper spiritual insights, greater peace, and a stronger sense of divine guidance. This is because listening creates space for God to speak, reveal His will, and lead you in ways that you might otherwise miss.

As you continue your fast, remember that listening is not just a passive activity but a deliberate choice to focus on God's presence, be still, and wait for His voice. By cultivating a listening heart, you are opening yourself to the transformative work of the Holy Spirit, who will guide you, comfort you, and lead you into deeper truth.

> **DAY 17 TIP: WATER FOR EMOTIONAL BALANCE AND INNER CALM**

On Day 17 of your twenty-one-day fast, staying hydrated plays a key role in supporting the emotional stability and calmness you're experiencing. Drinking water helps regulate body systems that influence mood, such as blood pressure and stress hormone levels, which can enhance your sense of inner peace and resilience. Dehydration can sometimes lead to irritability or fatigue, so keep water close by and sip steadily throughout the day to maintain both mental and emotional balance. By staying hydrated, you support not only your physical health but also the emotional clarity and stability that fasting brings at this stage, helping you feel centered and calm as you approach the final stretch of your fast.

JOURNALING: **REFLECTING ON LISTENING**

Journaling today provides an opportunity to reflect on the role of listening in your fasting journey. Use this time to document your thoughts, prayers, and any insights you receive about how listening is shaping your spiritual and emotional well-being.

JOURNALING PROMPTS:

1) How are you hearing God's voice during this fast? Reflect on any specific moments or insights where you've sensed God speaking to you. How is fasting helping you to listen more intently to His voice?

_____

_____

_____

_____

_____

_____

2) What distractions do you need to set aside to hear God more clearly? Consider the noise and busyness in your life that might be hindering your ability to listen to God. How can you create more space for stillness and listening?

_____

_____

_____

3) How does the scientific understanding of mindfulness enhance your spiritual practice? Think about how the cognitive benefits of mindfulness align with the spiritual practice of listening to God. How can you use this knowledge to deepen your ability to hear His voice during your fast?

4) What prayers of listening are on your heart today? Write out a personal prayer asking God to help you develop a listening heart. Ask for the patience, focus, and clarity needed to hear His voice and to respond with faith.

Journaling helps you to capture the spiritual and emotional benefits of listening during your fast. It's a way to document your journey, reflect on the growth you're experiencing, and deepen your connection with God through the practice of mindful listening.

ENCOURAGEMENT FOR THE JOURNEY AHEAD

As you conclude Day 17, take a moment to appreciate the profound impact that listening to God has on your fasting journey. In the stillness and quietness of fasting, you are creating a space where God's voice can be heard more clearly, where His guidance can become more evident, and where His presence can be more deeply felt. Listening is not just about hearing; it's about attuning your heart to God's frequency, aligning your will with His, and responding with trust and obedience.

As you continue your fast, let listening be a cornerstone of your spiritual practice—a way to stay connected to God, discern His will, and experience the peace that comes from knowing you are being guided by His hand. Trust that as you listen, God is speaking, leading, and drawing you closer to His heart.

Each day of your fasting journey is an opportunity to refine your ability to hear God's voice and respond with faith. As you cultivate a listening heart, know that you are deepening your relationship with God and positioning yourself to receive His guidance and blessings.

> **LOOKING AHEAD: PREPARING FOR DAY 18**

Tomorrow, as you enter Day 18, the theme will shift to one of **perseverance**. Fasting is a journey that calls for endurance, and as you near the final stretch, the need for perseverance becomes even more crucial. On Day 18, you'll delve into how to maintain your focus, strength, and commitment—especially as the challenges of fasting may intensify.

As you prepare for tomorrow, ask God to strengthen your resolve, renew your spirit, and equip you with the perseverance needed to finish your fast with grace and determination. Trust that He is with you, empowering you and guiding you through every step of this journey.

CHAPTER 19

DAY 18

THE STRENGTH OF PERSEVERANCE

ENDURING TO THE END

Welcome to Day 18 of your fasting journey. By now, you've traveled far along this path, experiencing both the highs and lows that come with fasting. As you near the final stretch, one key virtue becomes increasingly important: **perseverance.** Perseverance is the ability to stay the course and maintain your commitment and focus, even when the challenges of fasting become more pronounced. Today's focus is on the strength of perseverance—how to harness the inner resolve and spiritual fortitude needed to complete your fast with purpose and determination.

Perseverance is more than just enduring hardship; it's about pushing through obstacles with faith and confidence in God's strength. Fasting, especially in its later stages, can test your resolve in profound ways, but it also offers the opportunity to develop a deep, unwavering trust in God's sustaining power. This chapter is dedicated to helping you tap into the strength of perseverance, stay focused on the spiritual rewards of your fast, and finish strong.

This chapter will guide you in understanding the importance of perseverance during fasting, how to cultivate it in moments of difficulty, and how to rely on God's strength to carry you through to the end.

> ## OVERVIEW OF DAY 18:
> ## EMBRACING THE CHALLENGE

The theme for Day 18 is embracing the challenge of perseverance—a mindset that refuses to give up, even when the journey becomes difficult. Fasting, by its nature, is a discipline that requires endurance. The initial enthusiasm may have waned, physical and emotional challenges may have surfaced, and the finish line might still seem distant. Yet, it is in these moments that perseverance is forged, and the true value of your fast is realized.

Perseverance is not just about surviving the fast; it's about thriving in it. It's about embracing the challenges as opportunities for growth, allowing them to refine your character and deepen your reliance on God. As you fast, you are not just abstaining from food; you are training your spirit to press on, stay the course, and reach the end with a sense of accomplishment and spiritual renewal.

Today is about recognizing the importance of perseverance, of pushing through the barriers that may arise, and of trusting that God will provide the strength you need to finish your fast well. As you do so, you'll find that perseverance not only helps you complete your fast but also strengthens your faith and character for the challenges ahead.

SCRIPTURE OF THE DAY: HEBREWS 12:1-2

"Therefore, since we are surrounded by such a great cloud of witnesses, let us throw off everything that hinders and the sin that so easily entangles. And let us run with perseverance the race marked out for us, fixing our eyes on Jesus, the pioneer and perfecter of faith. For the joy set before him he endured the cross, scorning its shame, and sat down at the right hand of the throne of God."—Hebrews 12:1-2

Today's scripture from Hebrews encourages us to run the race of faith with perseverance, looking to Jesus as our example and source of strength. This passage reminds us that perseverance is not about running aimlessly; it's about staying focused on the goal, throwing off anything that hinders us, and pressing on with determination.

As you meditate on this verse, consider what it means to "run with perseverance" in the context of your fast. What obstacles are you facing that need to be thrown off? How can you fix your eyes on Jesus and draw strength from His example?

Perseverance is a key ingredient in finishing well. Today, let this verse inspire you to stay the course focus on the joy set before you, and trust that God will carry you through to the finish line.

KEY THOUGHT: PERSEVERANCE IS A TEST OF FAITH.

Today's key thought is that perseverance is a test of faith. It's easy to stay committed when things are going well, but true perseverance is revealed in the face of difficulty. Fasting challenges you to continue pressing forward, even when your body is tired, your mind is weary, and the temptation to quit grows stronger.

Perseverance is about holding on to your faith, trusting that God's grace is sufficient for every moment, and believing that the spiritual rewards of your fast are worth the struggle. It's about understanding that every challenge is an opportunity to grow stronger, deepen your trust in God, and demonstrate your commitment to Him.

As you move through today, reflect on how perseverance is shaping your fasting journey. How is it helping you to push through the difficult moments and stay focused on the spiritual goals you've set? Embrace the power of perseverance, knowing that it is a key to unlocking the full potential of your fast.

> ## PRAYER PROMPT: **A PRAYER FOR ENDURANCE**

Today's prayer focus is on asking God for the endurance needed to complete your fast. This is an opportunity to acknowledge the challenges you're facing, ask for His strength to persevere, and trust that He will carry you through to the end.

PRAYER PROMPT:

"Father, I come to You today, acknowledging the challenges that have come with this fast. I confess that there are moments when I feel weary, when my resolve weakens, and when the temptation to give up is strong. But Lord, I know that You are my strength, and I ask for Your grace to persevere. Help me to throw off everything that hinders me and to run with perseverance the race You have set before me. Lord, I fix my eyes on Jesus, the pioneer and perfecter of my faith, and I trust that You will give me the endurance I need to finish this

fast well. Thank You for the strength that comes from You, for the faith that sustains me, and for the joy that is set before me. In Jesus's name, I pray. Amen."

> ### SCIENTIFIC INSIGHT: **CELLULAR REJUVENATION AND IMMUNE ENHANCEMENT**

KEYWORD DEFINITION: CELLULAR REJUVENATION

Cellular rejuvenation is the process through which cells undergo repair, renewal, and, in some cases, regeneration to restore their optimal function. Imagine it as your body's way of refreshing its cells, making them function as if they were "new." During fasting, cellular rejuvenation is supported by processes like autophagy, where cells clear out old, damaged components and recycle them. This natural cleanup helps cells work more efficiently, reducing the effects of aging and supporting overall health. Over time, cellular rejuvenation contributes to the body's ability to recover from stress, fight off disease, and maintain vitality.[34]

Your body is continuing to rejuvenate at a cellular level, with autophagy clearing out the last of the damaged cells and toxins. Your immune system is getting a boost, making you more resilient to illness.

At this stage in your fast, your body is in a remarkable state of cellular rejuvenation. With digestion taking a back seat, your cells are dedicating energy to deep repair and renewal processes. Through autophagy, cells identify and recycle damaged components, which not only enhances their function but also reduces the cellular "clutter" that can accumulate with age. This process of cellular rejuvenation supports the health of tissues throughout your body,

---

[34] Kafi N. Ealey et al., "Intermittent fasting promotes rejuvenation of immunosenescent phenotypes in aged adipose tissue," *GeroScience* 46, no. 3 (2024): 3457-70, https://doi.org/10.1007/s11357-024-01093-4.

from skin to organs, helping you feel revitalized at a fundamental level. The effects extend beyond the fast, contributing to long-term resilience against aging and illness. On Day 18, your body is essentially hitting the "refresh" button at the cellular level, reinforcing the benefits of fasting in ways that can support vitality and wellness far into the future. Embrace this phase as a powerful moment of renewal, one that aligns your physical health with the deep rejuvenation fasting offers. Keep persevering; the end is in sight.

The Psychological and Physical Benefits of Perseverance

Perseverance, while often viewed as a mental and spiritual discipline, also has significant psychological and physical benefits. Research has shown that the ability to persevere through challenges can lead to improved mental health, increased resilience, and better overall well-being.

Perseverance is closely linked to mental resilience—the ability to cope with stress and adversity. Individuals who exhibit perseverance, often referred to as grit, are more likely to achieve long-term goals, experience lower levels of stress, and maintain a positive outlook even in difficult circumstances. This mental resilience is particularly important during fasting when physical and emotional challenges can arise.

Perseverance helps you to stay focused on your goals, push through moments of weakness, and maintain a sense of purpose even when the journey becomes difficult. This resilience not only benefits your fasting journey but also equips you to handle other life challenges with greater confidence and stability.

As you continue your fast, remember that perseverance is not just about enduring hardship; it's about embracing the challenges as opportunities for growth, relying on God's strength, and trusting that the spiritual rewards will far outweigh the temporary discomforts.

> **DAY 18 TIP: HYDRATION TO MAXIMIZE CELLULAR REJUVENATION**

On Day 18 of your twenty-one-day fast, hydration is essential to support the cellular rejuvenation your body is undergoing. Drinking water helps flush out the byproducts released as your cells recycle old components, aiding in detoxification and keeping this renewal process efficient. Staying hydrated also keeps you energized, preventing fatigue as your body devotes energy to deep repair. Sip water regularly throughout the day to maximize these rejuvenating benefits—this simple act supports the profound healing and revitalization happening within your body as you move closer to the completion of your fast.

> **JOURNALING: REFLECTING ON PERSEVERANCE**

Journaling today provides an opportunity to reflect on the role of perseverance in your fasting journey. Use this time to document your thoughts, prayers, and any insights you receive about how perseverance is shaping your spiritual and emotional well-being.

JOURNALING PROMPTS:

1) What challenges are you facing as you near the end of your fast? Reflect on the specific difficulties that have arisen during your fast. How are you responding to these challenges, and how is perseverance helping you to stay the course?

_____

_____

_____

2) How is perseverance strengthening your faith and character? Consider how pushing through the tough moments of your fast is deepening your trust in God and refining your character. How is perseverance helping you to grow spiritually?

3) How does the scientific understanding of perseverance enhance your spiritual practice? Think about how the psychological and physical benefits of perseverance align with the spiritual discipline of fasting. How can you use this knowledge to stay focused and committed as you approach the end of your fast?

4) What prayers of perseverance are on your heart today? Write out a personal prayer asking God to help you persevere through the remaining days of your fast. Ask for the strength, focus, and determination needed to finish well.

Journaling helps you to capture the spiritual and emotional benefits of perseverance during your fast. It's a way to document your journey, reflect on the growth you're experiencing, and deepen your connection with God through the practice of perseverance.

ENCOURAGEMENT FOR THE JOURNEY AHEAD

As you conclude Day 18, take a moment to recognize the strength and determination that perseverance brings to your fasting journey. Perseverance is not just about pushing through; it's about pushing forward—toward the goal, the reward, and the deeper relationship with God that awaits you. Each step you take, each moment you endure, is a testament to your faith and your commitment to God's purposes.

As you continue your fast, let perseverance be the driving force that keeps you focused, determined, and steadfast. Trust that as you press on, God is with you, providing the strength and grace you need to complete your fast with integrity and joy.

Each day of your fasting journey is an opportunity to grow stronger in faith and character. As you embrace perseverance, know that you are not just enduring; you are advancing—toward the spiritual breakthroughs and blessings that God has in store for you.

LOOKING AHEAD: PREPARING FOR DAY 19

Tomorrow, as you step into Day 19, the focus will shift to the theme of **renewal**. As you approach the final days of your fast, the concept of renewal becomes especially meaningful—renewal of mind, body, and spirit. On Day 19, you'll explore how fasting can lead to a refreshed sense of purpose, vitality, and spiritual clarity.

As you prepare for tomorrow, invite God to begin a work of renewal in your heart and mind. Ask Him to restore your strength and fill you with His Spirit as you near the completion of this journey. Trust that with each passing day, He is with you—renewing, refreshing, and guiding you as you continue on this path of transformation.

CHAPTER 20

DAY 19

THE GIFT OF RENEWAL

EMBRACING NEW BEGINNINGS

Welcome to Day 19 of your fasting journey. You are now in the final stretch, where the fruits of your perseverance are beginning to ripen, and the theme of renewal takes center stage. Renewal is a profound and beautiful aspect of fasting—an invitation to shed old patterns, refresh your spirit, and step into a new season with a renewed sense of purpose and vitality. Today, we focus on the gift of renewal—how fasting can restore your mind, body, and spirit, preparing you for the future God has for you.

Renewal is central to the Christian life, symbolizing the continual process of being made new in Christ. Fasting is a powerful catalyst for this renewal, as the physical act of abstaining from food reflects the spiritual act of letting go of the old and embracing the new. This chapter will guide you through understanding how fasting brings about renewal, how to welcome this transformation into every area of your life, and how to carry this renewed energy and clarity into the days beyond your fast.

Take this opportunity to embrace the renewal that fasting offers. Reflect on the areas of your life that are being made new, and trust in God's ability to transform every part of your being. As you move forward, may you carry this sense of renewal, knowing that it will continue to shape and bless your journey long after your fast has ended.

> ## OVERVIEW OF DAY 19:
> ## THE POWER OF BEING MADE NEW

The theme for Day 19 is the power of being made new—a concept that speaks to the heart of what it means to follow Christ. Renewal is not just about starting over; it's about being transformed, refreshed, and revitalized by the Spirit of God. As you near the end of your fast, you may begin to notice a shift—a renewed clarity of mind, a refreshed sense of purpose, and a revitalized connection with God.

Fasting is a journey that strips away the old, allowing space for the new to emerge. Whether it's a new mindset, a renewed commitment to God's will, or a fresh perspective on your life's purpose, the renewal that fasting brings is a gift to be embraced and cherished.

Today is about recognizing the areas in your life where God is bringing renewal, celebrating the newness that is emerging, and committing to carrying this renewal with you as you transition out of your fast. As you do so, you'll find that this sense of renewal not only energizes you for the final days of your fast but also sets the stage for the new season ahead.

The Gift of Renewal

> **SCRIPTURE OF THE DAY: ISAIAH 40:31**

"But those who hope in the LORD will renew their strength. They will soar on wings like eagles; they will run and not grow weary, they will walk and not be faint."—Isaiah 40:31

Today's scripture from Isaiah speaks to the promise of renewal for those who place their hope in the Lord. This verse is a powerful reminder that renewal comes not from our own efforts, but from God's strength, which lifts us up, refreshes our spirit, and gives us the endurance to continue the journey.

As you meditate on this verse, consider how God is renewing your strength during this fast. Are there areas where you feel revitalized, both physically and spiritually? How is God preparing you to soar on wings like eagles, run without growing weary, and walk without fainting?

Renewal is a promise that God offers to those who trust in Him. Today, let this verse encourage you to embrace the renewal that God is bringing into your life, rest in His strength, and look forward with hope to the new things He is doing.

> **KEY THOUGHT: RENEWAL IS A DIVINE GIFT.**

Today's key thought is that renewal is a divine gift—a gift that God bestows upon those who seek Him with a willing and open heart. Fasting creates a unique environment for this renewal, as it clears away the distractions and burdens that often weigh us down, allowing God's Spirit to refresh and revitalize every aspect of our being.

Renewal is not something we can manufacture on our own; it is the work of the Holy Spirit, who breathes new life into us, restores our strength, and prepares us for the path ahead. As you fast, you are opening yourself to this divine gift, inviting God to make all things new in your life.

As you move through today, reflect on the ways that God is bringing renewal into your life. How is He restoring your strength, renewing your mind, and refreshing your spirit? Embrace the gift of renewal, knowing that it is a sign of God's ongoing work in your life, preparing you for the next chapter of your journey.

> **PRAYER PROMPT: A PRAYER FOR RENEWAL**

Today's prayer focus is on asking God to renew your strength, your mind, and your spirit. This is an opportunity to receive the gift of renewal with gratitude, invite God to refresh every area of your life, and commit to carrying this renewal with you beyond the fast.

PRAYER PROMPT:

"Lord, I come to You today with a heart open to the renewal that only You can bring. I thank You for the strength You have given me during this fast, and I ask that You continue to renew my spirit as I approach the final days. Lord, I ask that You refresh my mind, giving me clarity and focus. Renew my heart, filling it with Your love and peace. Renew my strength, so that I may soar on wings like eagles, run and not grow weary, and walk and not faint. Thank You for the gift of renewal, for making all things new in my life, and for preparing me for the journey ahead. I trust in Your promise to renew me, and I embrace the newness that You are bringing into my life. In Jesus's name, I pray. Amen."

SCIENTIFIC INSIGHT: PREPARATION FOR RE-ENTRY

KEYWORD DEFINITION: RENEWAL

Renewal is the body's ability to restore and revitalize itself, replacing old or worn-out cells with new ones and restoring optimal function across systems. This concept is like giving your body a "reset," where cells, tissues, and organs are maintained in good health through a continuous cycle of repair and replacement. During fasting, renewal processes are activated as your body enters a state of deep maintenance and repair, breaking down and recycling damaged components and supporting cellular health. This renewal contributes to long-term resilience, helping the body stay youthful, functional, and better equipped to handle physical and environmental stresses.

As your fast nears its end, your body is preparing for the reintroduction of food. Digestive enzymes are starting to activate, and your metabolism is getting ready to handle a gradual increase in food intake.

By now, nineteen days in, your body is fully immersed in a powerful state of renewal. With digestion no longer demanding constant energy, your body channels its resources toward deep repair and rejuvenation. Cellular renewal—where old or damaged cells are replaced with new, healthier ones—is a key part of this process. Through mechanisms like autophagy, cells clear out dysfunctional parts, paving the way for improved function and vitality. This state of renewal goes beyond cellular repair; it's a holistic reset that can benefit your organs, immune system, and overall resilience.

As your body renews itself at a cellular level, you may notice a sense of refreshment not only physically but mentally and emotionally as well. Fasting enhances this renewal by activating pathways that protect against oxidative stress and reduce inflammation, which are critical for long-term health. By giving your body this time and space to renew itself, you're supporting greater vitality and resilience that can extend well beyond the fast. You're nearing the final stretch of your journey, and each moment is an opportunity to embrace the deep, restorative power of renewal happening within.

As you're in the final lap of your fast, you may notice that your mind becomes clearer, your thoughts more focused, and your ability to discern God's will more acute. This mental clarity is a direct result of the renewal process, where the distractions and noise of everyday life are stripped away, allowing you to think and perceive more clearly.

As you continue your fast, embrace the renewal that God is bringing into your life. This renewal is a sign of His ongoing work in you, preparing you for the new things He has in store. By welcoming this renewal, you are allowing God to refresh your spirit, renew your mind, and restore your strength for the journey ahead.

> ## DAY 19 TIP:
> ## HYDRATION TO ENHANCE DEEP RENEWAL

On Day 19 of your twenty-one-day fast, staying hydrated is essential to fully support your body's renewal processes. Drinking water aids in flushing out the byproducts that are released as your cells go through intense repair and rejuvenation, making sure these toxins don't linger. Proper hydration also sustains the energy and mental clarity that many people experience at this stage of fasting. Keep water nearby and consider drinking it slowly throughout the day to maintain a steady level of hydration. By supporting your body with water, you enhance the deep renewal that fasting brings to every cell, helping you feel refreshed and ready for the final days of your fast.

JOURNALING: **REFLECTING ON RENEWAL**

Journaling today provides an opportunity to reflect on the role of renewal in your fasting journey. Use this time to document your thoughts, prayers, and any insights you receive about how renewal is shaping your spiritual and emotional well-being.

JOURNALING PROMPTS:

1) In what areas of your life are you experiencing renewal? Reflect on the specific ways that God is bringing renewal into your life during this fast. How is He refreshing your mind, restoring your strength, and renewing your spirit?

_____

_____

_____

_____

_____

_____

2) How is renewal preparing you for the next season of your life? Consider how the renewal you are experiencing is equipping you for the challenges and opportunities that lie ahead. How is God using this time of renewal to prepare you for what is to come?

_____

_____

_____

3) How does the scientific understanding of renewal enhance your spiritual practice? Think about how the physical and psychological benefits of renewal align with the spiritual renewal you are experiencing. How can you use this knowledge to deepen your sense of renewal during your fast?

4) What prayers of renewal are on your heart today? Write out a personal prayer expressing your desire for renewal in every area of your life. Ask God to continue His work of renewal in you, refreshing your mind, body, and spirit as you approach the final days of your fast.

_____

_____

_____

_____

Journaling helps you to capture the spiritual and emotional benefits of renewal during your fast. It's a way to document your journey, reflect on the growth you're experiencing, and deepen your connection with God through the process of being made new.

ENCOURAGEMENT FOR THE JOURNEY AHEAD

As you conclude Day 19, take a moment to celebrate the renewal that God is bringing into your life through this fast. Renewal is not just about physical restoration; it's about a deep, spiritual refreshment that touches every part of your being. This renewal is a gift—a sign that God is at work in your life, preparing you for the new season that lies ahead.

As you continue your fast, let renewal be the theme that carries you through the final days. Trust that as you embrace this renewal, God is equipping you with the strength, clarity, and vitality needed to finish your fast with joy and step into the future with confidence.

Each day of your fasting journey is an opportunity to experience the gift of renewal in a deeper way. As you allow God to renew your mind, body, and spirit, know that you are being prepared for greater things, refreshed and revitalized for the road ahead.

> **LOOKING AHEAD: PREPARING FOR DAY 20**

Tomorrow, as you move into Day 20, the focus will shift to the theme of gratitude. As you near the completion of your fast, gratitude becomes a powerful way to reflect on the journey you've undertaken, celebrate the growth you've experienced, and give thanks for the many ways God has moved in your life during this time. On Day 20, you'll explore how to cultivate a heart of gratitude and how this practice can deepen your spiritual life even after the fast has ended.

As you prepare for tomorrow, ask God to fill your heart with gratitude, help you recognize the blessings of this journey, and give you the words to express your thanks. Trust that He is with you, guiding you, and blessing you as you draw closer to the end of your fast.

CHAPTER 21

DAY 20

THE GRACE OF GRATITUDE

Welcome to Day 20 of your fasting journey. You have come so far, navigating the challenges and joys of fasting with faith and perseverance. As you approach the conclusion of this journey, one theme emerges as essential: **gratitude**. Gratitude is more than just a polite "thank you;" it is a profound spiritual practice that aligns your heart with God's goodness and opens the door to deeper joy and peace. Today, we focus on the **grace of gratitude**—how cultivating a heart of thankfulness can transform your perspective, deepen your relationship with God, and enrich your spiritual life long after the fast ends.

Gratitude is a response to the recognition of God's blessings in your life. It's about acknowledging the countless ways He has provided, guided, and sustained you throughout this fasting journey. As you give thanks, you not only honor God but also position yourself to receive more of His grace and love. This chapter is dedicated to helping you embrace the practice of gratitude, view your fasting journey through the lens of thankfulness, and carry this spirit of gratitude with you into the days ahead.

This chapter will guide you in understanding the importance of gratitude, how to cultivate it during fasting, and how it can continue to shape your spiritual life beyond the fast.

> **OVERVIEW OF DAY 20:**
> **CULTIVATING A SPIRIT OF GRATITUDE**

The theme for Day 20 is cultivating a spirit of gratitude—a practice that has the power to transform your outlook on life. Gratitude shifts your focus from what you lack to what you have, from the challenges you've faced to the blessings you've received. As you near the end of your fast, reflecting on this journey with a heart of thankfulness can bring a sense of completion and fulfillment.

Gratitude is not about ignoring difficulties or pretending that everything is perfect; it's about choosing to see God's hand at work in all things, even in the challenges. As you fast, gratitude helps you to recognize the spiritual growth you've experienced, the ways God has spoken to you, and the strength you've gained. It allows you to celebrate the progress you've made and to look forward with hope and anticipation.

Today is about embracing gratitude as a way of life, not just a momentary feeling. It's about making thankfulness a regular part of your spiritual practice, allowing it to deepen your connection with God and to bring joy into every aspect of your life.

> **SCRIPTURE OF THE DAY: 1 THESSALONIANS 5:16-18**

"Rejoice always, pray continually, give thanks in all circumstances; for this is God's will for you in Christ Jesus."—1 Thessalonians 5:16-18

Today's scripture from 1 Thessalonians is a powerful reminder of the central place that gratitude holds in the Christian life. Paul encourages believers to rejoice always, pray continually, and give thanks in all circumstances, recognizing that these practices are part of God's will for us.

As you meditate on this verse, consider how you can incorporate gratitude into every aspect of your life. Are there specific moments during your fast where you've seen God's provision and guidance? How can you give thanks for these experiences, even if they were challenging at the time?

Gratitude is a choice, a discipline that aligns us with God's will. Today, let this verse inspire you to embrace a spirit of thankfulness, rejoice in all that God has done, and carry this gratitude with you beyond the fast.

> **KEY THOUGHT:**
> **GRATITUDE TRANSFORMS PERSPECTIVE.**

Today's key thought is that gratitude transforms perspective. When you choose to focus on what you are thankful for, you begin to see your life through the lens of God's grace. Gratitude shifts your attention from what is missing to what is present, from what is challenging to what is possible. It opens your eyes to the many ways God is working in your life and fills your heart with joy and contentment.

Fasting is a practice that can reveal both your strengths and your weaknesses, your joys and your struggles. By embracing gratitude, you allow yourself to see the growth and blessings that have come from this journey, celebrate the progress you've made, and thank God for His faithfulness.

As you move through today, reflect on how gratitude is shaping your fasting experience. How is it helping you to see God's hand at work in your life? How is it bringing you closer to Him? Embrace the power of gratitude, knowing that it has the ability to transform your heart, your mind, and your life.

PRAYER PROMPT: **A PRAYER OF THANKSGIVING**

Today's prayer focus is on offering a prayer of thanksgiving, expressing your gratitude to God for all that He has done during your fast. This is an opportunity to thank Him for the blessings, the lessons, and the growth you've experienced, and to commit to carrying this spirit of gratitude with you beyond the fast.

PRAYER PROMPT:

"Father, I come to You today with a heart full of gratitude. I thank You for the strength You've given me during this fast, for the ways You've guided me, and for the growth I've experienced. Lord, I am grateful for the challenges that have refined my faith, for the moments of clarity that have deepened my understanding, and for the peace that comes from being in Your presence. I thank You for Your provision, for Your grace, and for the love that sustains me each day. Help me to carry this spirit of gratitude with me beyond this fast, to rejoice always, to pray continually, and to give thanks in all circumstances. Thank You for being faithful, for being present, and for being my strength. In Jesus's name, I pray. Amen."

SCIENTIFIC INSIGHT: **SPIRITUAL AND PHYSICAL RENEWAL**

KEYWORD DEFINITION: GRATITUDE

Gratitude is the practice of recognizing and appreciating the positive aspects of life, from small moments to meaningful relationships. On a scientific level, gratitude has a powerful impact on mental and physical health by activating brain regions associated with reward, fostering positive emotions, and reducing stress. Expressing gratitude can increase dopamine and serotonin levels—neurotransmitters linked to happiness and well-being—helping create a more resilient and positive mindset. This practice also promotes heart health, reduces stress hormone levels, and can enhance overall life satisfaction, providing both emotional and physiological benefits.[35]

Your body is at the peak of its renewal process, with cellular repair and autophagy maximizing your health. Mentally and emotionally, you're likely feeling more stable and clear-headed than ever before.

The Psychological Benefits of Gratitude

Gratitude, while deeply spiritual, also has significant psychological benefits. Research has shown that cultivating a habit of thankfulness can lead to improved mental health, greater emotional resilience, and enhanced overall well-being.[36]

The Role of Gratitude in Emotional Well-Being

Gratitude is closely linked to emotional well-being. Individuals who regularly practice gratitude experience higher levels of happiness, lower levels of depression, and greater overall life satisfaction. Gratitude shifts your focus from negative emotions and thoughts to positive ones, creating a more optimistic and hopeful outlook on life.

During fasting, when you may be more attuned to your emotions, practicing gratitude can help you to navigate any challenges or difficulties with a sense of peace and contentment. It allows you to see the good in every situation and to find joy in the journey, even when it's difficult.

---

35 Robert A. Emmons and Charles M. Shelton, "Gratitude and the Science of Positive Psychology" in *Handbook of Positive Psychology,* eds. C. R. Snyder and Shane J. Lopez (Oxford University, 2002), 459-71.
36 Robert A. Emmons and Anjali Mishra, "Why Gratitude Enhances Well-Being: What We Know, What We Need to Know," in *Designing Positive Psychology: Taking Stock and Moving Forward,* eds. Kennon M. Sheld, Todd B. Kashdan, and Michael F. Steger (Oxford University, 2011), 248-62.

By practicing gratitude, you are equipping yourself with the emotional tools needed to persevere through difficult moments, maintain a sense of balance and perspective, and emerge from the fast with a renewed sense of strength and purpose.

Gratitude during fasting can lead to profound spiritual growth. Gratitude, when practiced regularly, can deepen your spiritual life, increase your sense of connection with God, and enhance your overall sense of purpose and meaning. This is because gratitude aligns your heart with God's will, opening you to His blessings and allowing you to experience His presence in new and powerful ways.

As you continue your fast, embrace gratitude as a central part of your spiritual practice. By focusing on what you are thankful for, you are inviting God to work more deeply in your life, transform your heart, and fill you with His joy and peace.

DAY 20 TIP: HYDRATION TO SUPPORT FINAL DETOX AND MENTAL CLARITY

On Day 20 of your twenty-one-day fast, hydration remains crucial as your body enters the final stages of detox and renewal. Drinking water helps your system flush out any remaining toxins and supports the cellular repair processes that have been active throughout your fast. Staying well-hydrated today also enhances mental clarity, helping you maintain focus and a calm mindset as you approach the finish line. Keep water nearby and sip consistently to ensure you're fully supporting this powerful phase of your fast—hydration now sets the stage for the complete rejuvenation you'll experience on Day 21.

JOURNALING: **REFLECTING ON GRATITUDE**

Journaling today provides an opportunity to reflect on the role of gratitude in your fasting journey. Use this time to document your thoughts, prayers, and any insights you receive about how gratitude is shaping your spiritual and emotional well-being.

JOURNALING PROMPTS:

1) What are you most grateful for during this fast? Reflect on the specific blessings, growth, and experiences that have stood out to you during your fasting journey. How has God shown His faithfulness to you during this time?

_____
_____
_____
_____
_____
_____
_____

2) How is gratitude transforming your perspective on your fast? Consider how focusing on thankfulness is changing the way you view your fasting experience. How is it helping you to see the positive aspects of the journey, even in the midst of challenges?

_____
_____

3) How does the scientific understanding of gratitude enhance your spiritual practice? Think about how the psychological benefits of gratitude align with the spiritual practice of thankfulness. How can you use this knowledge to deepen your sense of gratitude during your fast?

4) What prayers of thanksgiving are on your heart today? Write out a personal prayer expressing your gratitude to God for all that He has done during your fast. Thank Him for His blessings, His guidance, and His presence in your life.

_____

_____

_____

_____

Journaling helps you to capture the spiritual and emotional benefits of gratitude during your fast. It's a way to document your journey, reflect on the growth you're experiencing, and deepen your connection with God through the practice of thankfulness.

ENCOURAGEMENT FOR THE JOURNEY AHEAD

As you conclude Day 20, take a moment to immerse yourself in the grace of gratitude. Gratitude is more than just a response to blessings; it is a way of life that opens your heart to God's goodness and aligns your spirit with His will. Through gratitude, you are acknowledging the countless ways God has been present in your fasting journey, sustaining you, guiding you, and blessing you.

As you continue your fast, let gratitude be the song of your heart—a melody of thankfulness that echoes through every moment of your day. Trust that as you give thanks, God is drawing you closer to Himself, filling you with His joy, and preparing you for the abundant life He has in store. Each day of your fasting journey is an opportunity to deepen your practice of gratitude, celebrate the growth you've experienced, and give thanks for the many ways God has moved in your life. As you embrace gratitude, know that you are stepping into a life filled with God's grace and blessings.

LOOKING AHEAD: **PREPARING FOR DAY 21**

Tomorrow, as you move into Day 21, the focus will shift to the theme of reflection and celebration. The final day of your fast is a time to look back on the journey you've undertaken, celebrate the progress you've made, and give thanks for the ways God has transformed your life. On Day 21, you'll explore how to reflect on your fasting experience with a heart of gratitude and how to celebrate the completion of this spiritual journey.

As you prepare for tomorrow, ask God to give you a heart of celebration, help you reflect on the journey with joy, and fill you with a sense of accomplishment and peace as you conclude your fast. Trust that He is with you, guiding you, and rejoicing with you as you complete this sacred journey.

CHAPTER 22

DAY 21

REFLECTION AND CELEBRATION

THE JOURNEY TO COMPLETION

Welcome to Day 21 of your fasting journey. You've reached the final day, a significant milestone in your spiritual walk. Today is a day of reflection and celebration—a time to look back on the journey you've undertaken, recognize the growth and transformation you've experienced, and celebrate the completion of this sacred practice. The culmination of your fast is not just about reaching the end; it's about acknowledging the work God has done in you and embracing the new beginnings that lie ahead.

Reflection is a vital part of any spiritual journey. It allows you to process your experiences, see how far you've come, and recognize the lessons learned along the way. Celebration, on the other hand, is an expression of joy and gratitude, a way of honoring the hard work, dedication, and spiritual breakthroughs that have marked your fast. This chapter is dedicated to helping you reflect on your fasting journey with a heart of gratitude and celebrate the completion of this transformative experience.

This chapter will guide you in reflecting on the key moments of your fast, how to celebrate the spiritual growth you've achieved, and how to carry the lessons learned into your life beyond the fast.

> ## OVERVIEW OF DAY 21: REFLECTING ON THE JOURNEY

The theme for Day 21 is reflecting on the journey—a practice that invites you to pause, look back on the path you've traveled, and recognize the significant moments that have shaped your fast. Reflection is not just about recalling events; it's about understanding the deeper meaning behind your experiences, seeing God's hand in every step, and acknowledging the growth that has taken place.

Celebration naturally follows reflection. As you recognize the spiritual victories, the challenges overcome, and the insights gained, you are moved to celebrate the work God has done in your life. Celebration is a way of giving thanks, marking the completion of this journey with joy and gratitude, and stepping into the next season with renewed strength and purpose. Today is about embracing the dual practices of reflection and celebration, allowing them to bring closure to your fasting journey and to set the stage for the new beginnings that await you.

> ## SCRIPTURE OF THE DAY: PHILIPPIANS 1:6

> *"Being confident of this, that he who began a good work in you will carry it on to completion until the day of Christ Jesus."*—Philippians 1:6

Today's scripture from Philippians speaks to the assurance that God, who began a good work in you, will carry it on to completion. This verse is a powerful reminder that the spiritual growth and transformation you've experienced during your fast are part of a larger journey—a journey that God is faithfully guiding.

As you meditate on this verse, consider how God has been at work in your life during this fast. What are the specific ways He has begun a good work in you? How can you trust that He will continue this work, carrying it to completion as you move forward? Reflection allows you to see the continuity of God's work in your life, from the beginning of your fast to its completion and beyond. Today, let this verse inspire you to trust in God's ongoing work, celebrate the progress you've made, and look forward with confidence to the future.

> **KEY THOUGHT:**
> **REFLECTION DEEPENS UNDERSTANDING.**

Today's key thought is that reflection deepens understanding. By taking the time to reflect on your fasting journey, you gain a deeper appreciation for the experiences you've had, the lessons you've learned, and the ways God has been at work in your life. Reflection allows you to see the bigger picture, understand the significance of each moment, and recognize the growth that has taken place.

Celebration flows naturally from this reflection. As you look back with gratitude, you are moved to celebrate the completion of your fast, rejoice in the spiritual victories you've achieved, and give thanks for the grace that has carried you through. Reflection and celebration together create a sense of closure and fulfillment, marking the end of your fast with joy and purpose. As you move through today, reflect on the key moments of your fasting journey. How has God been at work in your life? What lessons have you learned, and how have you grown? Embrace the power of reflection, knowing that it deepens your understanding and enriches your celebration.

> **PRAYER PROMPT:**
> **A PRAYER OF REFLECTION AND CELEBRATION**

Today's prayer focus is on reflecting on your fasting journey with gratitude and celebrating the work God has done in your life. This is an opportunity to thank God for His faithfulness, acknowledge the growth you've experienced, and commit to carrying the lessons learned into the future.

PRAYER PROMPT:

"Father, I come to You today with a heart full of gratitude as I reflect on this fasting journey. I thank You for the strength You've given me, for the guidance You've provided, and for the growth I've experienced. Lord, I celebrate the work You've done in my life during this fast—the lessons learned, the challenges overcome, and the spiritual victories achieved. I thank You for beginning a good work in me, and I trust that You will carry it on to completion. As I conclude this fast, I commit to carrying these lessons with me, to continue growing in faith, and to trust in Your ongoing work in my life. Thank You for Your faithfulness, Your love, and Your grace. In Jesus's name, I pray. Amen."

> **SCIENTIFIC INSIGHT:**
> **BODY SYSTEMS OPTIMIZATION**

Congratulations! You've reached the final day of your fast. Your body's systems are fully optimized, and you're ready to start reintroducing food carefully.

During the fast, your body has undergone significant transformation and optimization across its systems. By reducing the demands of constant digestion, your body redirected its energy towards repairing and enhancing core systems—boosting cellular renewal, increasing mitochondrial efficiency, and strengthening immune resilience. Autophagy, the body's natural "clean-up" process, has helped clear out damaged cells and optimize cellular function, setting the stage for improved vitality. Hormonal balance has also been recalibrated, supporting better mood stability, mental clarity, and metabolic health. Today, as you conclude this journey, your body stands rejuvenated, more efficient, and better equipped to maintain health and energy. Embrace this moment of optimization, as it reflects the cumulative benefits of your dedication, laying a strong foundation for continued wellness and vitality in the days ahead. To conclude the fasting adventure in a way that sets you up to sustain the gains of your fast, for now, let's focus on reflection and celebration!

The Role of Reflection in Personal Growth

Reflection is a powerful tool for personal growth and self-awareness. Notably, individuals who regularly engage in reflective practices experience greater self-understanding, improved decision-making, and increased emotional intelligence. Reflection allows you to process your experiences, learn from them, and integrate those lessons into your life.

During fasting, reflection helps you to understand the deeper significance of your journey, see how you've grown, and recognize the areas where God has been at work. It also provides a sense of closure, allowing you to appreciate the progress you've made and prepare for the next steps in your spiritual journey.

Celebration and Emotional Well-Being

Celebration, on the other hand, is closely linked to emotional well-being. Those who regularly celebrate their achievements, both big and small, experience higher levels of happiness, reduced stress, and greater overall life satisfaction. Celebration allows you to acknowledge your successes, take pride in your accomplishments, and share your joy with others. As you conclude your fast, celebrating the journey you've undertaken can provide a sense of fulfillment and joy, reinforcing the positive aspects of your experience and motivating you to continue growing in your faith. Spiritual practices such as reflection and celebration enhance spiritual awareness, increase feelings of gratitude, and deepen one's sense of purpose and meaning. By reflecting on your fasting journey and celebrating its completion, you are not only honoring your commitment but also acknowledging God's presence and work in your life.

As you conclude your fast, take time to reflect on the journey you've undertaken, celebrate the growth you've experienced, and give thanks for the many ways God has blessed you. These practices will help you integrate the lessons learned into your daily life, continue growing in your faith, and carry the spirit of gratitude and joy into the future.

> ### DAY 21 FINAL TIP: **EMBRACE REFLECTION, CELEBRATION, AND A GENTLE TRANSITION**

As you prepare to reintroduce food, continue to drink water to support your body's adjustment. Take it slow—begin with light, easily digestible foods and allow your body time to reacclimate gradually. Spiritually, this is a time for celebration and reflection. You've completed a powerful journey, and this day isn't just an ending; it's the start of a new chapter. Reflect on the insights you've gained, the resilience you've built, and the growth you've experienced. Carry these lessons forward into your life. Today is a moment for gratitude, self-honor, and embracing all that lies ahead.

> ### JOURNALING: **REFLECTING ON THE JOURNEY AND CELEBRATING**

Journaling today provides an opportunity to reflect on your fasting journey and celebrate the growth and transformation you've experienced. Use this time to document your thoughts, prayers, and any insights you receive about how reflection and celebration are shaping your spiritual and emotional well-being.

JOURNALING PROMPTS:

1) What are the key moments of growth and transformation during your fast? Reflect on the significant experiences that have shaped your fasting journey. How have these moments contributed to your spiritual growth and understanding?

_____

_____

_____

_____

_____

_____

2) How does reflection deepen your understanding of your fasting journey? Consider how reflecting on your experiences helps you to see the bigger picture, understand the significance of each moment, and appreciate the growth you've achieved.

_____

_____

_____

_____

_____

_____

3) How does celebration enhance your sense of fulfillment and joy? Think about how celebrating the completion of your fast brings a sense of closure and fulfillment. How can you carry this spirit of celebration into the next season of your life?

___

4) What prayers of reflection and celebration are on your heart today? Write out a personal prayer thanking God for the journey you've undertaken, reflecting on the lessons learned, and celebrating the growth you've experienced.

___

Journaling helps you to capture the spiritual and emotional benefits of reflection and celebration during your fast. It's a way to document your journey, reflect on the growth you've experienced, and deepen your connection with God through the practices of reflection and celebration.

ENCOURAGEMENT FOR THE JOURNEY AHEAD

As you conclude Day 21, take a moment to reflect on the journey you've completed and celebrate the work God has done in your life. This fasting journey has been one of challenge, growth, and transformation, and now you stand at the threshold of a new beginning. Reflection allows you to see how far you've come, understand the significance of each step, and recognize the ways God has been at work in your life.

Celebration is your response to this reflection—a way of honoring the progress you've made, rejoicing in the victories achieved, and giving thanks for the grace that has carried you through. As you celebrate the completion of your fast, know that this is not the end, but a new beginning, a stepping stone to the next chapter of your spiritual journey.

Each day of your fasting journey has been an opportunity to grow closer to God, deepen your faith, and experience His presence in new and profound ways. As you reflect on and celebrate this journey, know that you are being prepared for the greater things that lie ahead, filled with God's strength, wisdom, and grace.

LOOKING AHEAD: **THE JOURNEY BEYOND THE FAST**

As you conclude your fast, the focus now shifts to the journey beyond. The lessons you've learned, the growth you've experienced, and the transformation that has taken place are not meant to be left behind—they are meant to carry you forward, guide you in your daily walk with God, and empower you to live out your faith with renewed purpose and passion. As you move beyond the fast, ask God to help you integrate these lessons into your daily life, continue growing in your relationship with Him, and walk in the strength and wisdom that He has imparted to you during this journey. Trust that He is with you, guiding you, and preparing you for the next steps in your spiritual journey.

CHAPTER 23

PREPARING FOR RE-ENTRY

OVERVIEW: REINTRODUCING FOOD AND NORMAL ACTIVITIES WITH WISDOM AND GRACE

Congratulations! You've completed your fast—a spiritual journey that has brought you closer to God, strengthened your faith, and helped you focus on what truly matters. This is no small feat, and now, as you prepare to re-enter normal life, it's essential to do so with the same intention and grace that guided you through the fast. Reintroducing food and returning to your normal activities is not just a physical process; it's a spiritual one, too. The way you approach this phase can help preserve the benefits you've gained from fasting and avoid any unnecessary discomfort. Your body has adapted to the fasting state, so it needs time to adjust to regular meals again. And just as importantly, your heart and mind need time to reflect on the lessons learned and integrate your new spiritual rhythms into daily life.

Think of this re-entry as a continuation of the fast—a way to honor the journey you've just completed. It's not about rushing back to "normal" but about stepping into the next phase with wisdom, patience, and grace. In this chapter, we'll walk through some practical steps for how to break your fast gradually. We'll also explore the spiritual insights that can help you carry the clarity and connection you've cultivated into everyday life. This is a moment to continue walking closely with God, allowing Him to guide you as you step forward with a renewed sense of purpose and peace.

> **SCRIPTURE OF THE DAY: ECCLESIASTES 3:1**

"There is a time for everything, and a season for every activity under the heavens."—Ecclesiastes 3:1

As you prepare to transition out of your fast, Ecclesiastes 3:1 reminds us that there is a time and a season for everything. Just as there was a time to fast, there is now a time to reintroduce food and normal activities. This scripture encourages you to embrace the season of re-entry with the same mindfulness and intentionality that you brought to your fast. It's a reminder that this process is part of God's plan for your spiritual growth, and it should be approached with wisdom and care.

Reflect on how this verse applies to your current season. How can you reintroduce food and activities in a way that honors the work God has done in you during your fast? How can you continue to live with the intentionality that you practiced during your fasting journey?

> **KEY THOUGHT: RE-ENTER NORMAL LIFE WITH THE SAME INTENTIONALITY AS WHEN YOU FASTED.**

Re-entry is not just a physical transition; it's a spiritual one as well. The same intentionality you brought to your fast should now guide your return to normal life. Consider the habits you've developed, the clarity you've gained, and the spiritual insights you've received. How can these be integrated into your daily routine?

Approach re-entry with mindfulness, taking it slow and allowing your body and spirit to adjust. Just as you were intentional about what you abstained from during your fast, be intentional about what you now reintroduce. This isn't a time to rush back into old patterns, but rather a time to thoughtfully consider how you can maintain the spiritual growth you've experienced.

> ### SCIENTIFIC INSIGHT: THE STRATEGY AND IMPORTANCE OF BREAKING THE FAST GRADUALLY

KEYWORD DEFINITION: GRADUALLY

"Gradually" refers to a process that unfolds in small, steady steps over time rather than occurring all at once. In the context of the body, gradual changes allow systems to adapt smoothly without being overwhelmed, whether it's in adjusting to new foods after a fast or building up endurance over time. For example, when reintroducing food after a prolonged fast, eating gradually helps the digestive system ease back into activity, preventing discomfort and allowing the body to absorb nutrients efficiently. Gradual processes are essential in many physiological adaptations because they support sustainable change without shocking the body's systems.

Breaking a fast requires careful planning. After a prolonged period without food, your digestive system needs time to readjust. Jumping back into regular eating too quickly can lead to discomfort, bloating, and other digestive issues. The key to successful re-entry is to break your fast gradually, starting with light, easily digestible foods.

Suggested Types of Easy Meals

1) Broth and Soups: Begin with clear vegetable or bone broth, which is gentle on the stomach and helps rehydrate your body. As you progress, you can add soft vegetables or pureed soups.
2) Fruits: Start with juicy fruits like watermelon, oranges, or cantaloupe. These are easy to digest and provide natural sugars to gently reintroduce carbohydrates into your system.
3) Steamed Vegetables: Lightly steamed vegetables like spinach, zucchini, or carrots are easy on the digestive system and provide necessary vitamins and minerals.
4) Yogurt and Kefir: These fermented dairy products are rich in probiotics, which can help restore your gut flora after fasting. Choose unsweetened versions to avoid unnecessary sugars.
5) Oatmeal or Porridge: A small serving of oatmeal or porridge can be a good way to reintroduce grains into your diet. Make it with water or a small amount of plant-based milk.

Remember, the goal is to reintroduce food slowly and to listen to your body. Eat small portions and take your time. Gradually, over the course of several days, you can start incorporating more solid foods and return to regular meals. There are more resources, expert advice, and community on the fasting companion app—you can download it on the Google Play Store and the App Store.

JOURNALING: PLAN YOUR TRANSITION AND REFLECT ON THE LESSONS LEARNED

Journaling today is an opportunity to plan your transition back to normal life and to reflect on the lessons you've learned during your fast. Use this time to think about how you want to approach re-entry, both physically and spiritually.

JOURNALING PROMPTS:

1) How will you reintroduce food gradually? Create a plan for the types of foods you will start with and how you will slowly build up to regular meals. Consider any challenges you might face and how you will overcome them.

___

2) What spiritual habits will you continue? Reflect on the spiritual practices that have been most meaningful to you during your fast. How can you integrate these into your daily routine going forward?

___

3) What lessons have you learned during this fast? Write down the key insights, lessons, and spiritual breakthroughs you've experienced. How will you carry these lessons with you as you re-enter normal life?

4) How will you maintain the intentionality of your fast in your daily life? Consider how you can continue to live with the same focus and purpose that you practiced during your fast. What changes will you make to ensure that the spiritual growth you've experienced continues?

Preparing for Re-entry **247**

———————————————————————
———————————————————————
———————————————————————
———————————————————————
———————————————————————
———————————————————————

Journaling helps you to create a thoughtful plan for re-entry, ensuring that you transition back to normal life in a way that honors your fasting journey and the work God has done in you.

LOOKING AHEAD: EMBRACING A NEW BEGINNING

As you complete your fast and begin the process of re-entry, remember that this is not just the end of a spiritual discipline but the beginning of a new chapter in your spiritual journey. The insights, growth, and clarity you've gained during this fast are now tools that you can carry with you into your daily life. Embrace this new beginning with the same intentionality and grace that have carried you through your fast, trusting that God will continue to guide and strengthen you as you move forward.

CHAPTER 24

A NEW BEGINNING

OVERVIEW: ENDING THE FAST AND EMBRACING THE NEW SPIRITUAL INSIGHTS AND HABITS YOU'VE GAINED

As your fast draws to a close, you stand on the threshold of a new beginning. This is a moment to celebrate not just the completion of the fast, but the transformation it has brought into your life. The spiritual insights, habits, and disciplines that you've developed during this period are now a part of you, ready to be carried forward into your daily walk with God.

Ending a fast is not simply about resuming normal eating or returning to everyday activities. It's about recognizing the growth you've experienced and embracing the new opportunities for spiritual and personal development that lie ahead. This chapter is dedicated to helping you transition into this new phase with a sense of purpose and intentionality, ensuring that the changes you've experienced during your fast continue to bear fruit in your life.

> **SCRIPTURE OF THE DAY: LAMENTATIONS 3:22-23**

"Because of the LORD's great love we are not consumed, for his compassions never fail. They are new every morning; great is your faithfulness."—Lamentations 3:22-23

Today's scripture from Lamentations reminds us of God's unfailing love and the new mercies He offers us each day. As you conclude your fast, this verse serves as a powerful reminder that each day is a new beginning, an opportunity to experience God's grace afresh. The end of your fast is not an end at all, but the start of a new chapter in your spiritual journey, filled with renewed purpose and divine possibilities.

As you meditate on this verse, consider how God's mercies have been evident in your fasting journey. How has He sustained you, guided you, and revealed His love to you? How can you carry this awareness of His new mercies into your daily life as you move forward?

> **KEY THOUGHT: THE END OF THE FAST IS A NEW BEGINNING IN YOUR SPIRITUAL JOURNEY.**

The end of your fast is a significant milestone, but it is also a new beginning. The spiritual growth, insights, and disciplines you've cultivated during this time are not meant to be left behind—they are the foundation for the next steps in your journey with God. This is a time to build on the momentum you've gained, continue seeking God with the same fervor, and embrace the new opportunities for growth that He is placing before you. This new beginning is an invitation to deepen your relationship with God, live out the spiritual insights you've gained, and continue growing in faith and purpose.

A New Beginning

As you move forward, remember that the end of the fast is not the end of your spiritual journey—it is the start of something new and beautiful.

> **PRAYER PROMPT: PRAY FOR GOD'S GUIDANCE AS YOU MOVE FORWARD WITH RENEWED PURPOSE**

As you transition into this new beginning, it's important to seek God's guidance and to commit your next steps to Him. This prayer prompt encourages you to ask for His direction, seek His wisdom, and move forward with a renewed sense of purpose and trust in His plan.

PRAYER PROMPT:

"Father, as I conclude this fast, I come before You with a heart full of gratitude for the journey You've led me on. I thank You for the growth, the insights, and the spiritual renewal I've experienced. Lord, I ask for Your guidance as I move forward into this new beginning. Help me to carry the lessons I've learned into my daily life, to continue seeking You with all my heart, and to live out the purpose You've placed within me. Father, I commit my next steps to You, trusting in Your wisdom and Your plan for my life. Lead me, guide me, and help me to walk in the newness of life that You have given me. In Jesus's name, I pray. Amen."

> ### SCIENTIFIC INSIGHT: THE BODY'S RETURN TO NORMAL EATING AND THE IMPORTANCE OF MAINTAINING HEALTHFUL PRACTICES

KEYWORD DEFINITION: MODERATION

Moderation is the practice of avoiding extremes and instead keeping behaviors or choices within healthy limits. In the context of health and fasting, moderation is essential—it means finding a balanced approach to eating, exercise, and other lifestyle factors without overindulging or depriving the body. Moderation helps maintain steady energy, supports mental well-being, and promotes sustainable habits. For instance, when breaking a fast, eating in moderation allows the digestive system to ease back into function, preventing strain and discomfort. Physiologically, moderation supports homeostasis, the body's internal balance, which is key to overall health and longevity.

As you reintroduce food after a fast, your body begins the process of returning to its normal metabolic state. This transition is crucial for maintaining the health benefits you've gained during your fast. While the temptation might be to indulge in rich, heavy foods, it's important to approach this phase with the same intentionality that you brought to the fast itself.

The Body's Adjustment to Normal Eating

After a prolonged fast, your digestive system has adapted to a lower intake of food. This means that sudden, heavy meals can be difficult for your body to process, leading to discomfort, bloating, and other digestive issues. To avoid this, it's important to gradually reintroduce food, starting with light, easily digestible meals, as mentioned in the previous chapter. Continuing to focus on whole, nutrient-dense foods, staying hydrated, and listening to your body's hunger cues will help you maintain the benefits of the fast. Moreover, consider maintaining some of the healthful practices you adopted during the fast, such as regular prayer, meditation, and mindful eating, as these will support both your spiritual and physical well-being.

Importance of Maintaining Healthful Practices

The end of a fast is an opportunity to evaluate your lifestyle and to make lasting changes that support your health and spiritual life. Consider integrating some of the beneficial habits you developed during your fast into your daily routine. Whether it's eating more mindfully, setting aside regular time for prayer and reflection, or continuing to focus on a diet rich in whole foods, these practices will help you maintain the gains you've made and continue growing in health and faith.

> **POST-FAST TIP: WATER FOR SMOOTH DIGESTION AND CONTINUED DETOX**

After completing your fast, staying hydrated is crucial for helping your body adjust to eating again. Drinking water supports digestion, allowing your stomach and intestines to process food gently and effectively as you reintroduce nutrients. Hydration also helps maintain the detox benefits achieved during your fast, flushing out any remaining toxins and keeping your body in a balanced state. Start each meal with a glass of water to prepare your digestive system and continue to sip throughout the day. This simple practice will make your transition smoother, keeping you refreshed and helping your body absorb nutrients optimally as you begin to eat again.

> ## JOURNALING: **REFLECT ON THE ENTIRE FASTING EXPERIENCE, HOW YOU'VE GROWN, AND YOUR NEXT STEPS**

Journaling today provides an opportunity to reflect on your entire fasting journey—how you've grown, the insights you've gained, and the ways God has worked in your life. Use this time to think about the next steps in your spiritual journey and how you can continue building on the foundation you've established during the fast.

JOURNALING PROMPTS:

1) How have you grown during this fast? Reflect on the specific areas of spiritual, emotional, and physical growth you've experienced. What changes have you noticed in your relationship with God, your self-discipline, and your overall well-being?

_____

_____

_____

_____

_____

2) What new spiritual insights have you gained? Consider the new perspectives, understandings, and revelations that have come to you during your fast. How will these insights shape your walk with God moving forward?

_____

_____

3) What are your next steps in your spiritual journey? Think about how you can continue to grow in faith and purpose now that the fast is ending. What habits, disciplines, or practices will you carry forward?

4) How can you maintain the healthful practices you've adopted? Reflect on the physical and spiritual practices that have benefited you during the fast. How will you integrate these into your daily life to maintain the progress you've made?

_____

_____

_____

_____

Journaling helps you to process the entire fasting experience, celebrate the growth you've experienced, and plan your next steps in your spiritual journey.

> ## LOOKING AHEAD:
> ## MOVING FORWARD AFTER THE FAST

As you conclude your fast and begin this new chapter in your spiritual journey, remember that the growth you've experienced and the insights you've gained are just the beginning. This new beginning is an opportunity to continue deepening your relationship with God, build on the foundation you've established, and live out the purpose He has placed within you. Embrace this new season with faith, intentionality, and a heart full of gratitude for all that God has done and will continue to do in your life.

CHAPTER 25

POST-FAST REFLECTIONS AND NEXT STEPS

> OVERVIEW: **REFLECTING ON THE TWENTY-ONE-DAY FAST AND ITS IMPACT ON YOUR LIFE**

As you come to the end of this 21-day fasting journey, it's important to take a moment to reflect on the profound impact it has had on your life. This period of fasting was not just about abstaining from food; it was about drawing closer to God, gaining clarity, deepening your spiritual walk, and experiencing transformation in every area of your life. As you reflect, you'll begin to see how God has been working in ways that you may not have noticed in the moment, but that are now evident as you look back.

Reflection helps solidify the spiritual lessons you've learned, and it creates a foundation for ongoing growth. By considering how this fast has shaped you—spiritually, emotionally, and physically—you can identify the areas where you've grown and those where God is calling you to continue developing. This chapter will guide you through a time of reflection, encourage you to plan your next steps and help you bring closure to this season with a sense of fulfillment and purpose.

TIPS FOR MAINTAINING SPIRITUAL DISCIPLINE AND HEALTH BENEFITS AFTER THE FAST

The benefits of this fast don't have to end here. With intentionality, you can maintain the spiritual discipline and health benefits you've gained. Here are some tips to help you continue growing:

1) Integrate Spiritual Disciplines into Your Daily Routine

The prayer, meditation, and Bible study practices that sustained you during the fast should remain a cornerstone of your spiritual life. Set aside time each day to continue these disciplines, ensuring that your relationship with God remains a priority. Consider joining a study group, finding a spiritual mentor, or committing to regular personal retreats to keep your spiritual life vibrant and growing.

2) Adopt Healthy Eating Habits

The focus on whole, nutrient-dense foods during your fast has likely contributed to a feeling of increased vitality and well-being. Continue to prioritize a balanced diet rich in fruits, vegetables, lean proteins, and whole grains. Staying mindful of what you consume and how it affects your body will help you maintain the physical benefits you've experienced during your fast.

3) Practice Prayer, God's presence and Gratitude

Prayer, presence, and gratitude were likely essential elements of your fasting experience. Continue to practice being present in each moment, whether in prayer, eating, or daily activities. Cultivate an attitude of gratitude, recognizing God's blessings in the small and significant aspects of your life. This mindset will help you maintain the peace and clarity you've gained during your fast.

4) Set New Spiritual Goals

The conclusion of your fast is the perfect time to set new spiritual goals. Whether it's a deeper study of Scripture, a commitment to serve others, or a focus on personal development, setting goals will help you continue to grow in your faith. Revisit these goals regularly and adjust them as God leads you.

ENCOURAGEMENT TO CONTINUE SEEKING GOD WITH THE SAME FERVOR

The passion and dedication with which you sought God during this fast should not diminish now that the fast is over. Instead, let this be the beginning of a deeper, more intentional walk with God. Continue to seek Him with the same fervor, trusting that He will continue to reveal Himself to you in new and profound ways. Remember, the spiritual growth you've experienced during this fast is not meant to be a temporary high; it is the foundation for a life of ongoing transformation and closeness with God.

Let this journey inspire you to pursue God with all your heart, soul, mind, and strength. As you move forward, remain open to His guidance, embrace the lessons He has taught you, and walk confidently in the path He has set before you.

> ## FINAL PRAYER AND COMMITMENT: **A PRAYER OF THANKSGIVING AND DEDICATION TO GOD**

As you conclude this fast, take a moment to offer a final prayer of thanksgiving and commitment. This prayer is a time to express your gratitude for the journey, acknowledge the work God has done in your life, and dedicate yourself to continuing the spiritual growth and discipline you have cultivated during this time.

FINAL PRAYER:

"Father, I thank You for guiding me through this twenty-one-day journey of fasting and seeking You. I am deeply grateful for the strength You have given me, the revelations You have provided, and the transformation You have brought into my life. As I conclude this fast, I commit myself to continuing the path of growth and closeness with You. Help me to carry the lessons I've learned into my daily life, to maintain the spiritual and health benefits I've gained, and to seek You with all my heart in every season of life. Lord, I dedicate my future to You, trusting that You will continue to lead me, mold me, and draw me closer to Your heart. Thank You for Your unwavering love, faithfulness, and presence in my life. In Jesus's name, I pray. Amen."

MOVING FORWARD AFTER THE FAST

As you step beyond this fast, remember that this journey doesn't end here. The spiritual growth, discipline, and deeper relationship with God that you've developed over these twenty-one days are just the beginning. They are the foundation upon which the rest of your spiritual life is built. Continue to seek God daily, nurture the spiritual disciplines you've embraced, and live out the purpose He has for you with a renewed sense of energy and focus.

This fasting experience has equipped you with valuable tools for ongoing growth. Whether it's through continued fasting, prayer, Bible study, or acts of service, stay committed to the journey of becoming more like Christ. The end of this fast is not the end of your spiritual walk—it's a new beginning, a launching point for a deeper and more intimate relationship with God.

Thank you for coming on this journey, and may you continue to grow in grace, wisdom, and faith as you move forward. Wishing you well as you step into all that God has in store for you ahead!

www.ingramcontent.com/pod-product-compliance
Lightning Source LLC
Chambersburg PA
CBHW050858160426
43194CB00011B/2197